PRESS RAPPEL

©2024 Rosaire Appel
Press Rappel
www.rosaireappel.com
ISBN: 9798872623441

# deaf poems

by Rosaire Appel

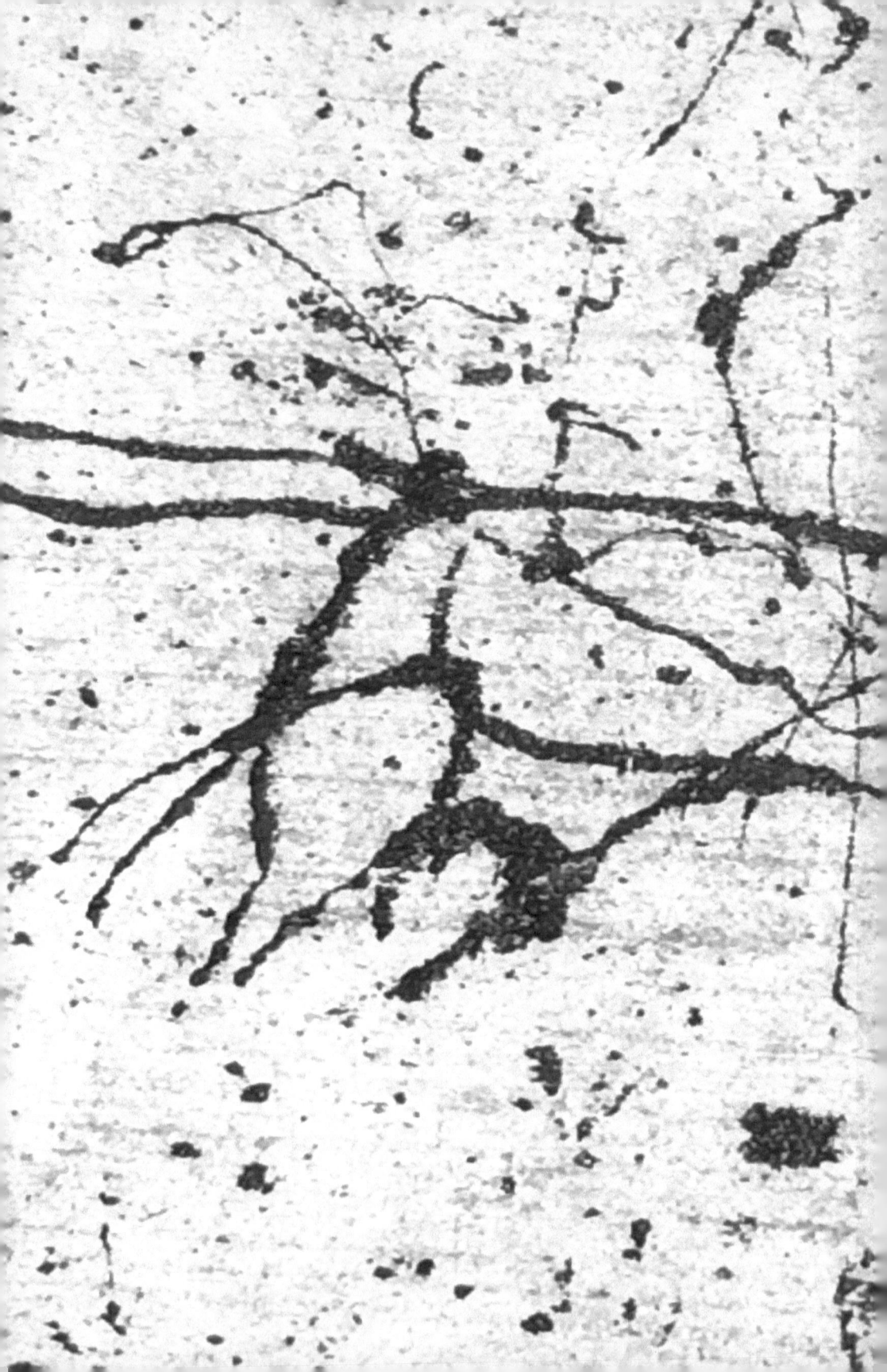

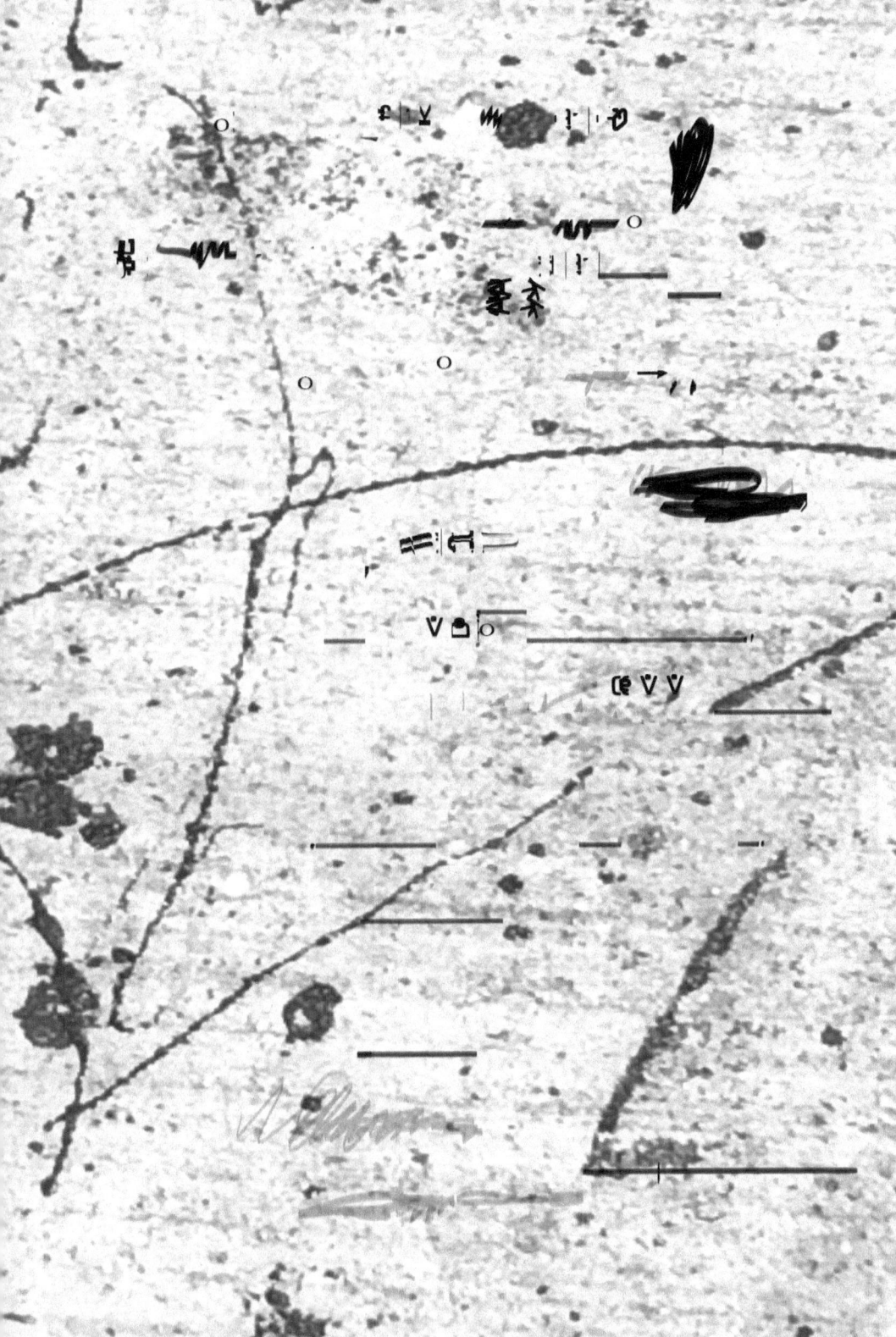

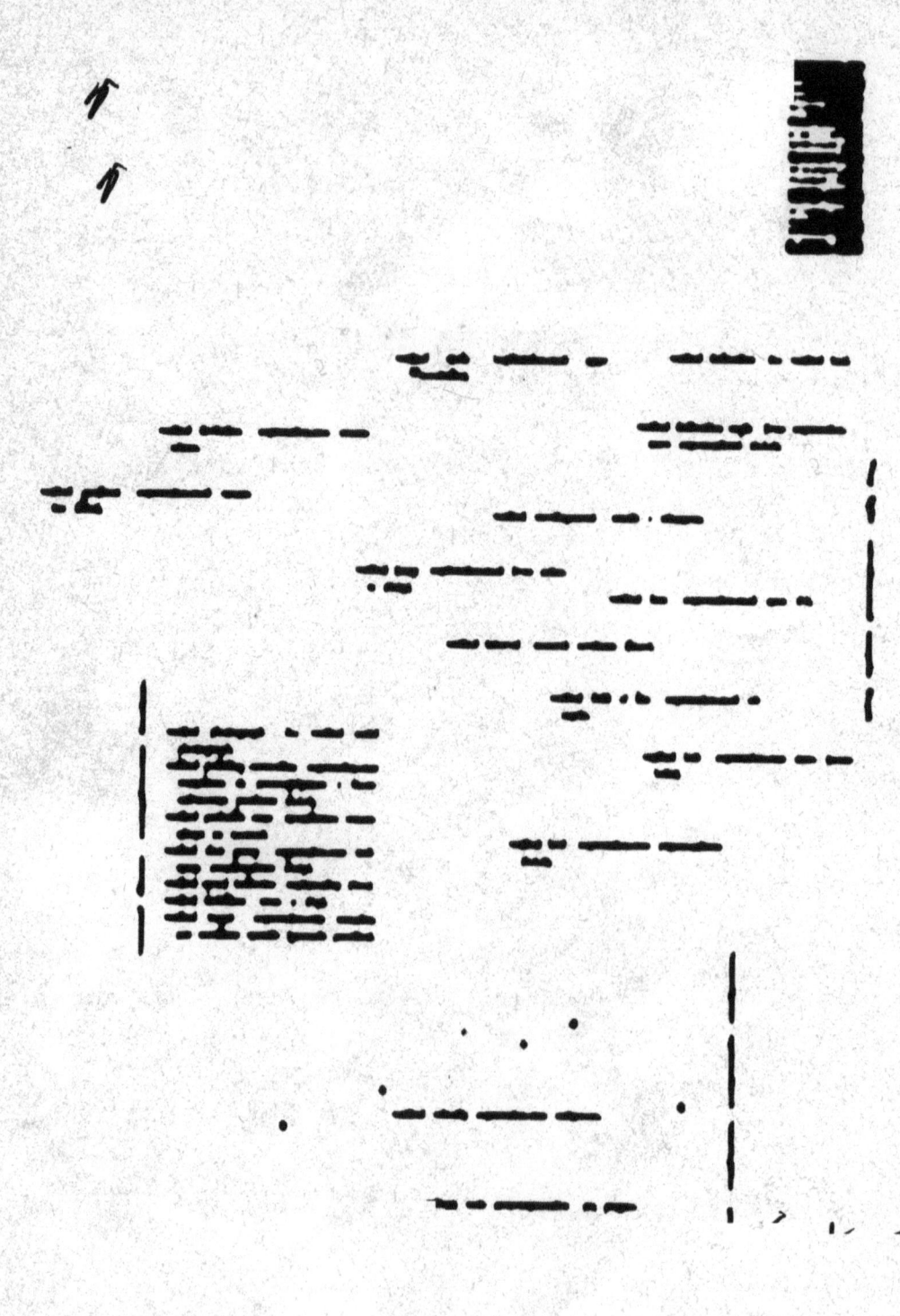

....these poems, they're deaf. Can't
hear me, or you for that matter.
Yet they call themselves poems. But-
what is a poem?
Who decides?

When the hand•knows what it's doing -
is there a problem?

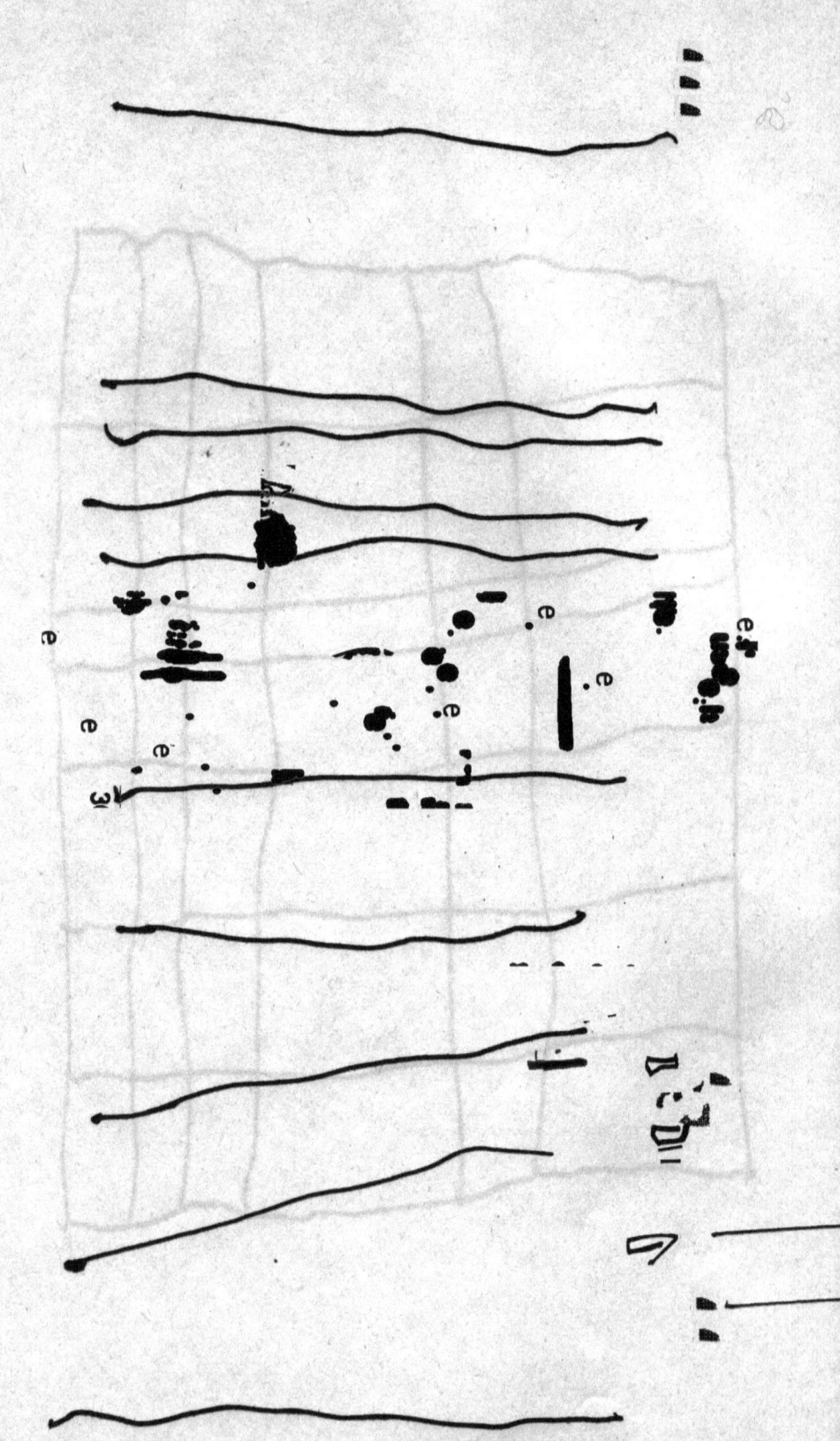

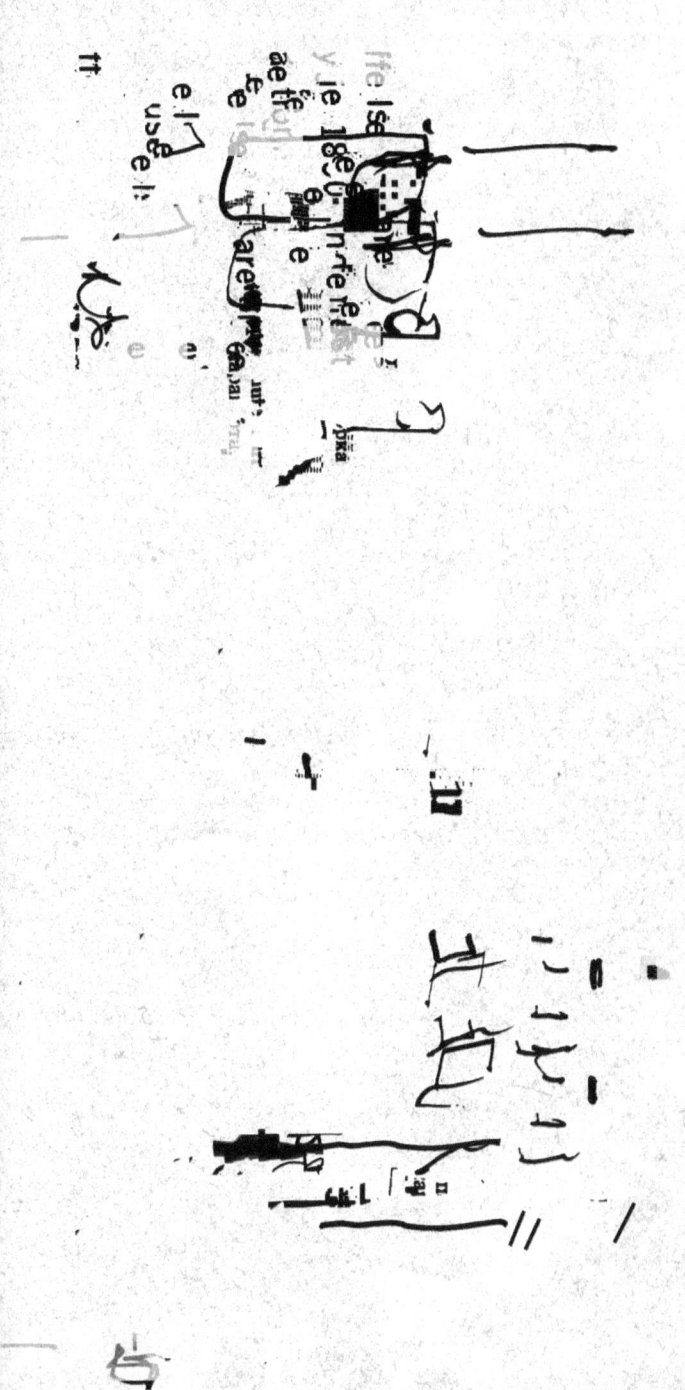

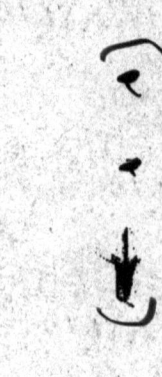

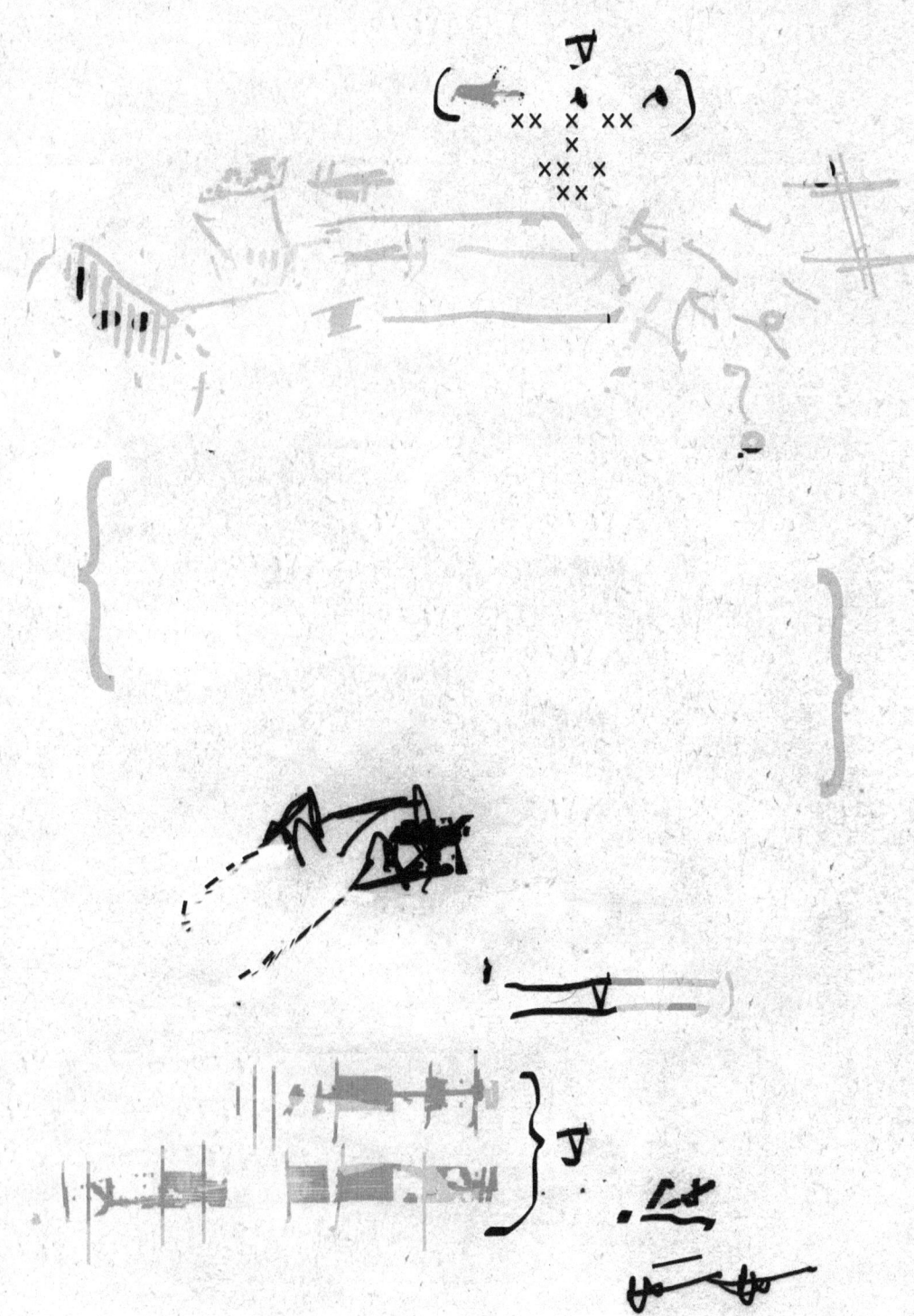

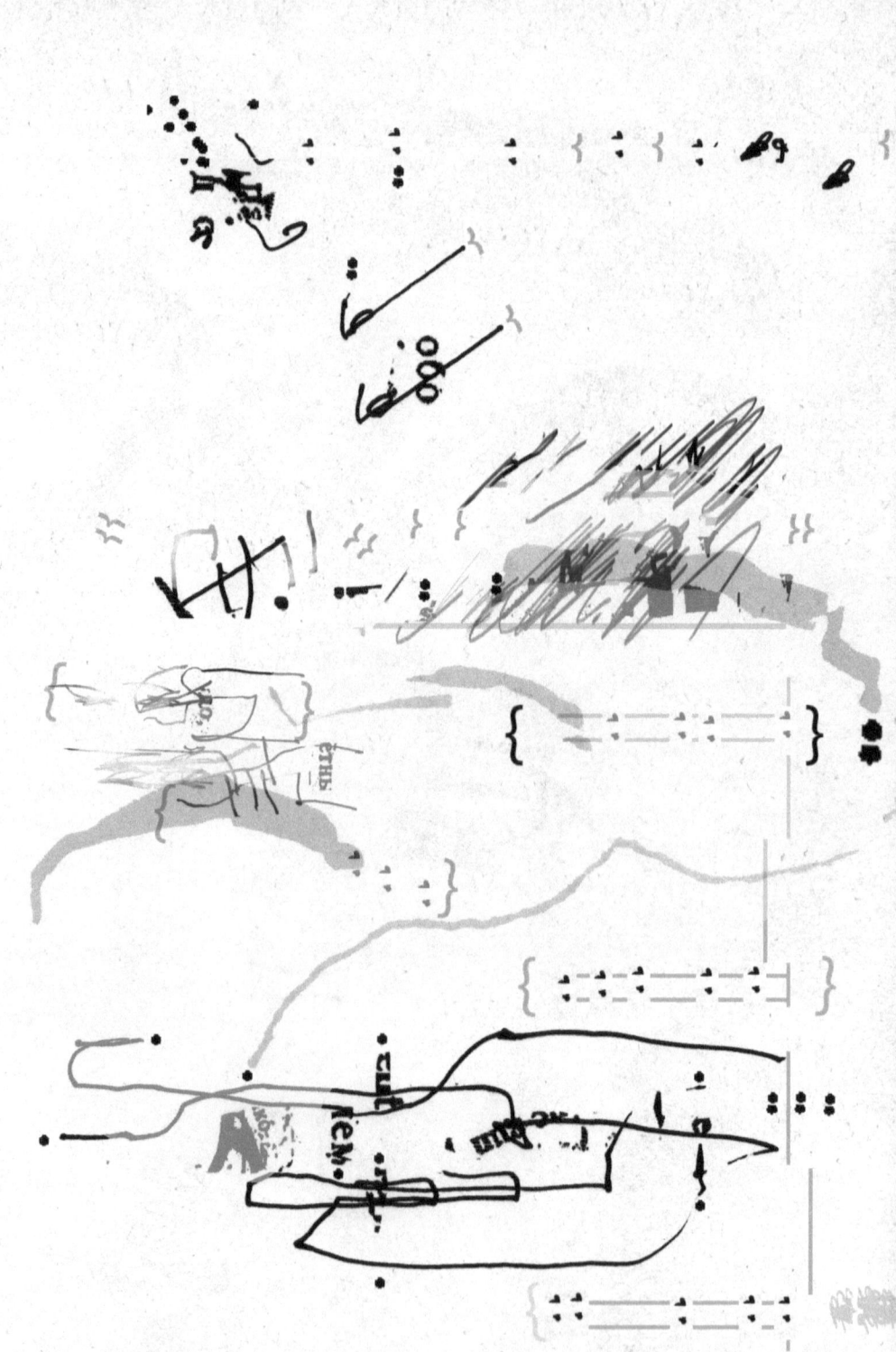

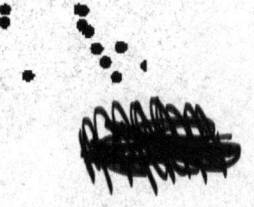

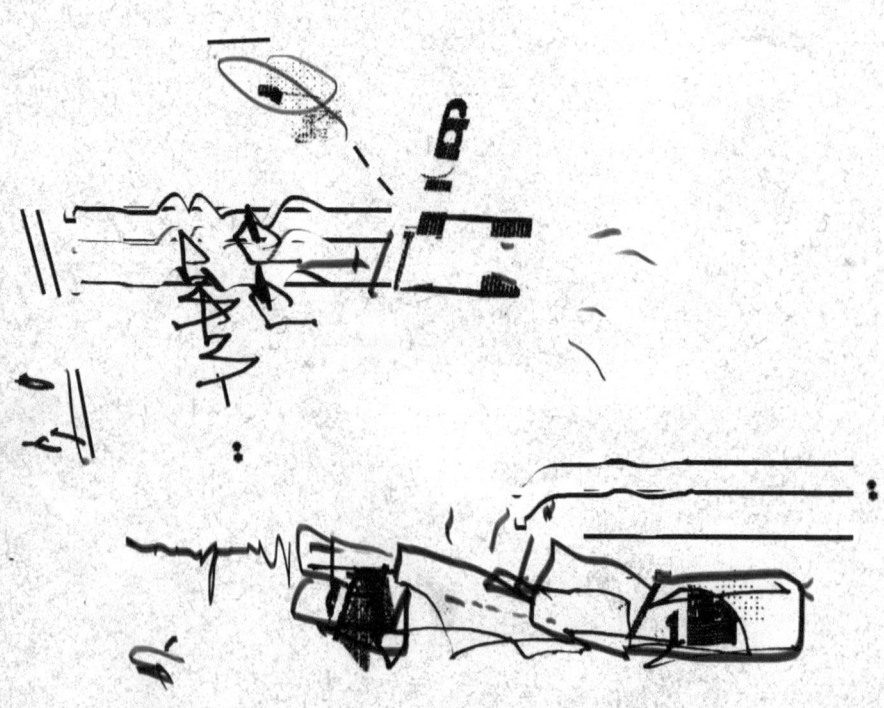

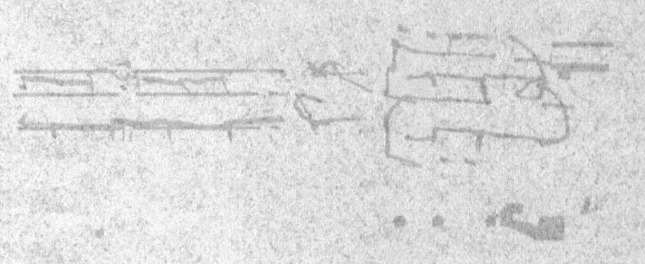

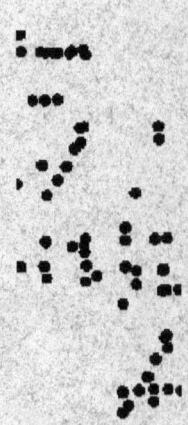

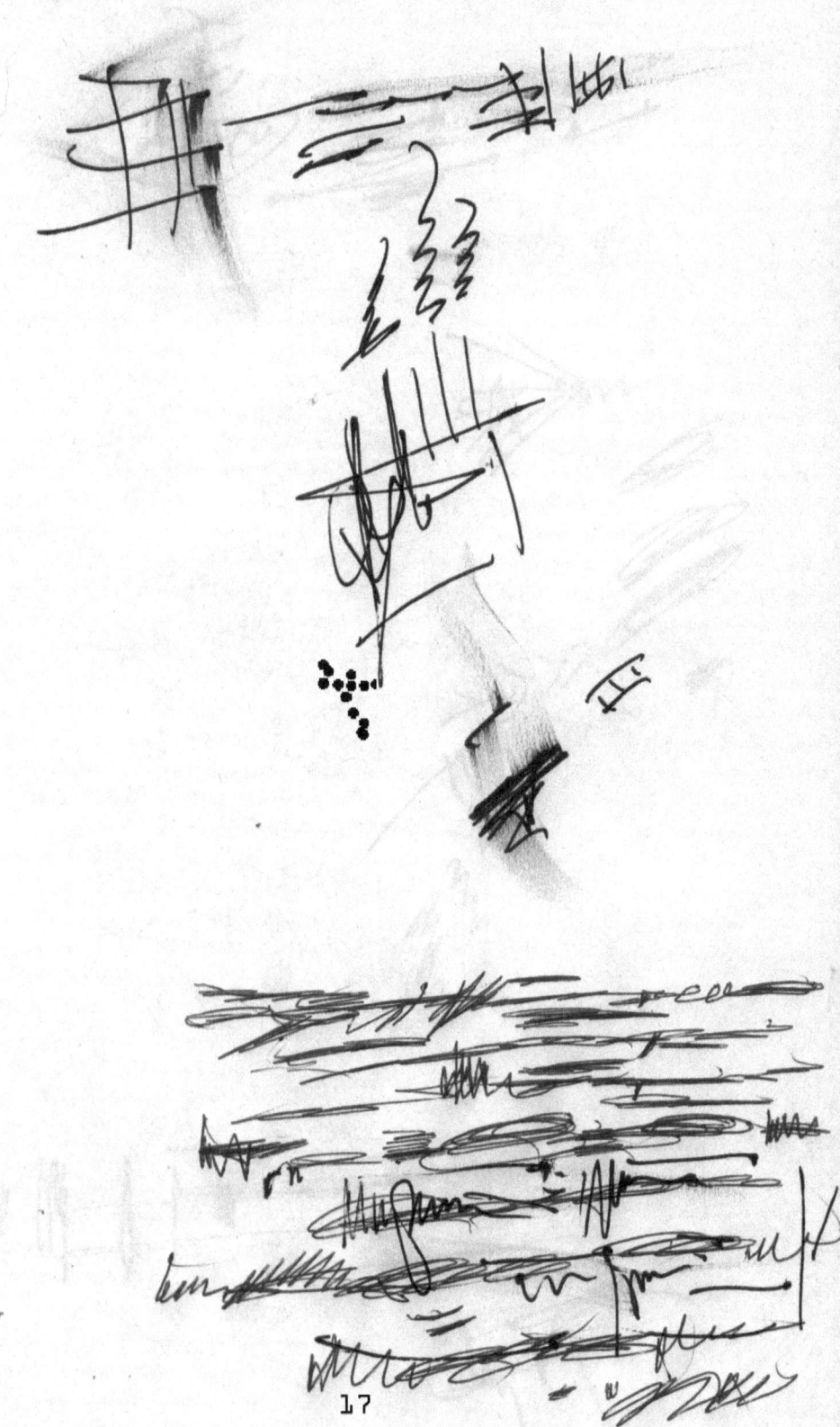

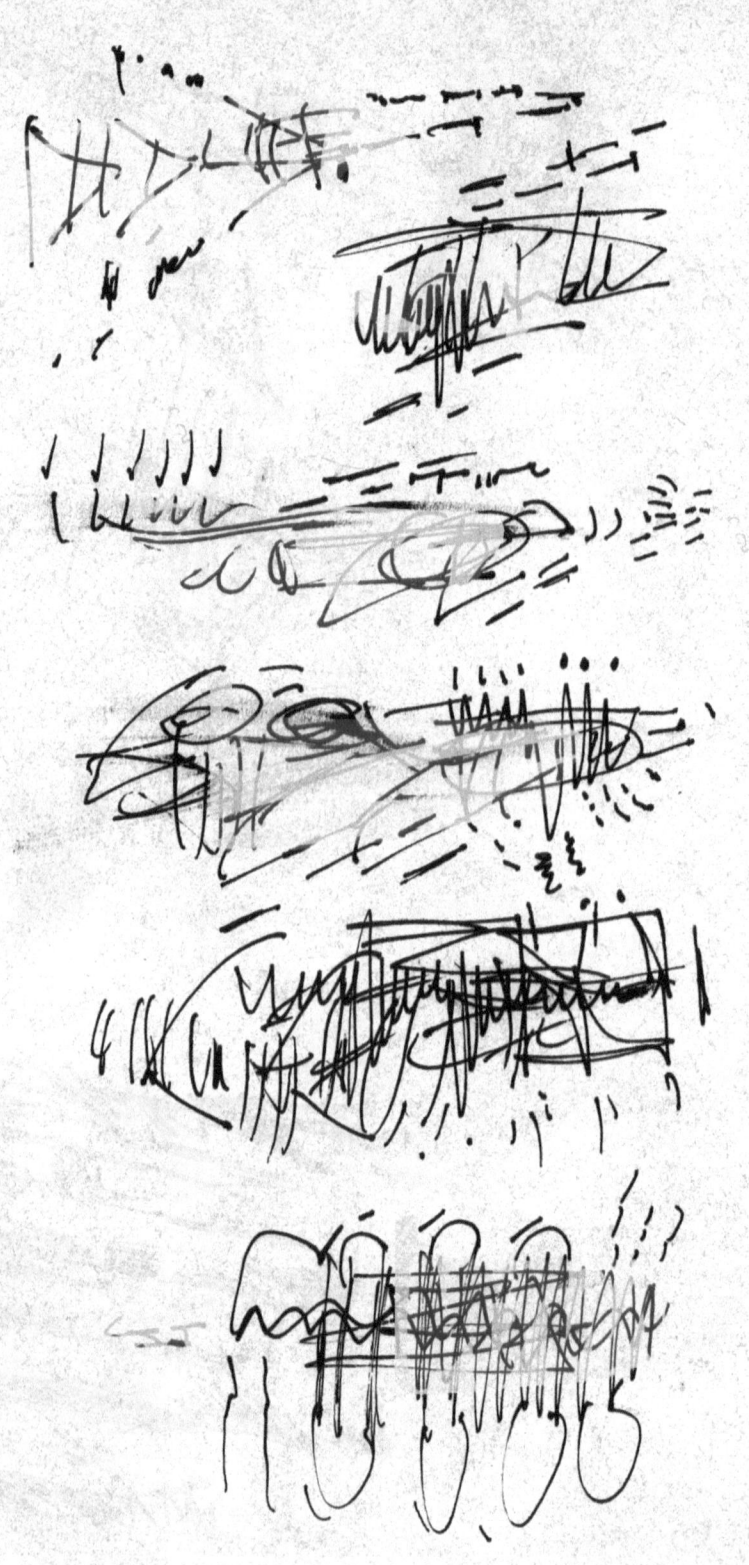

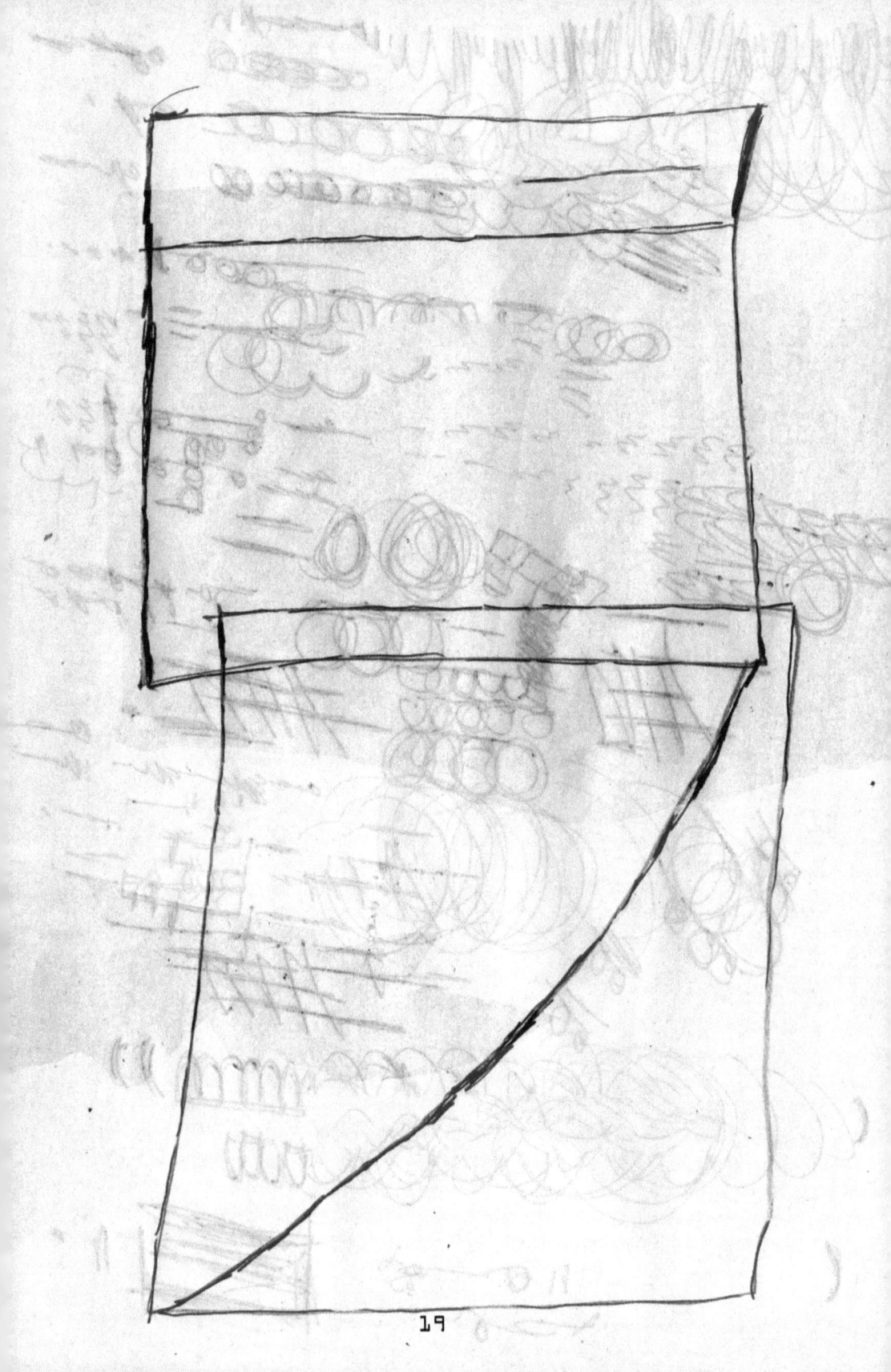

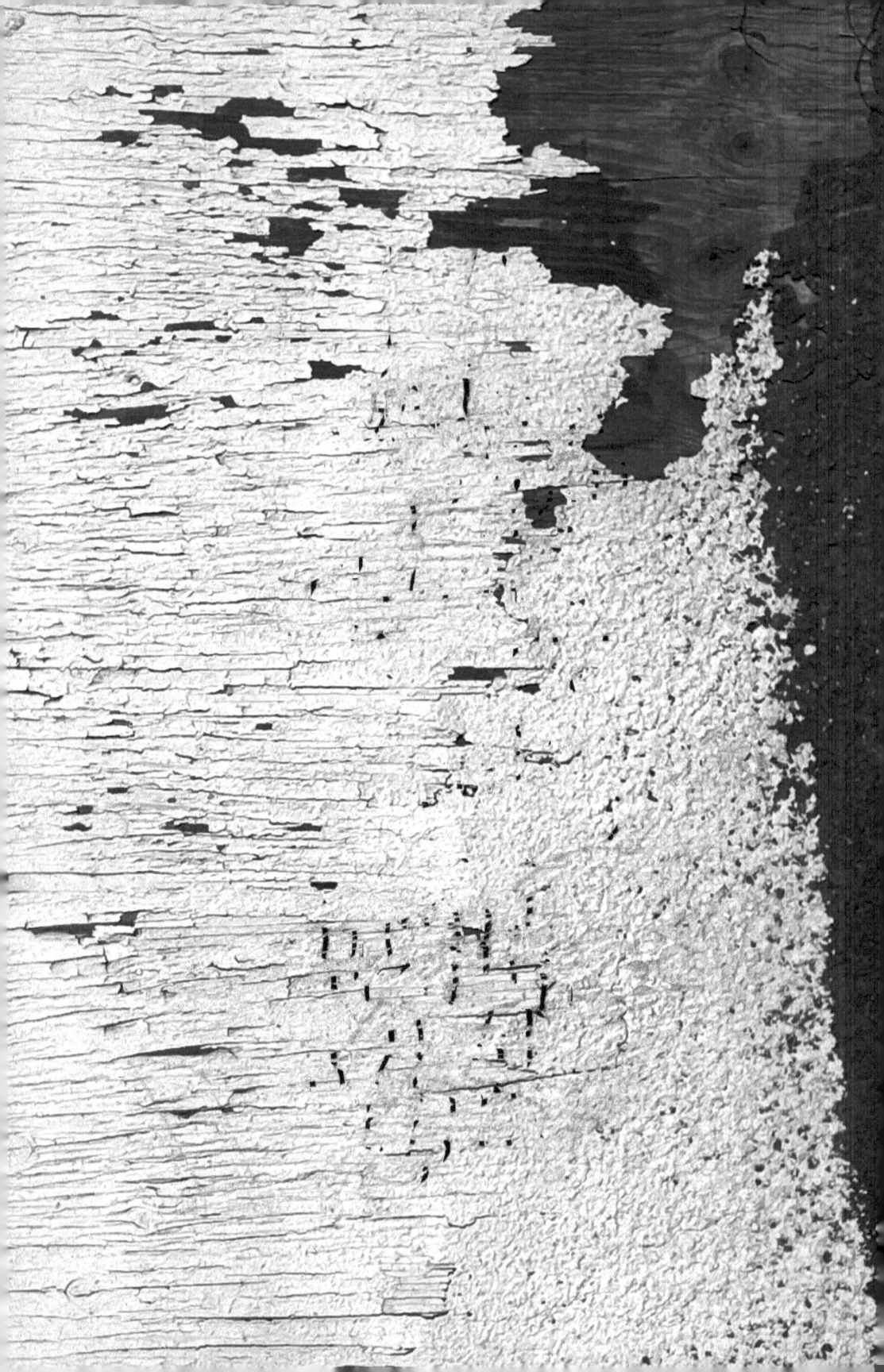

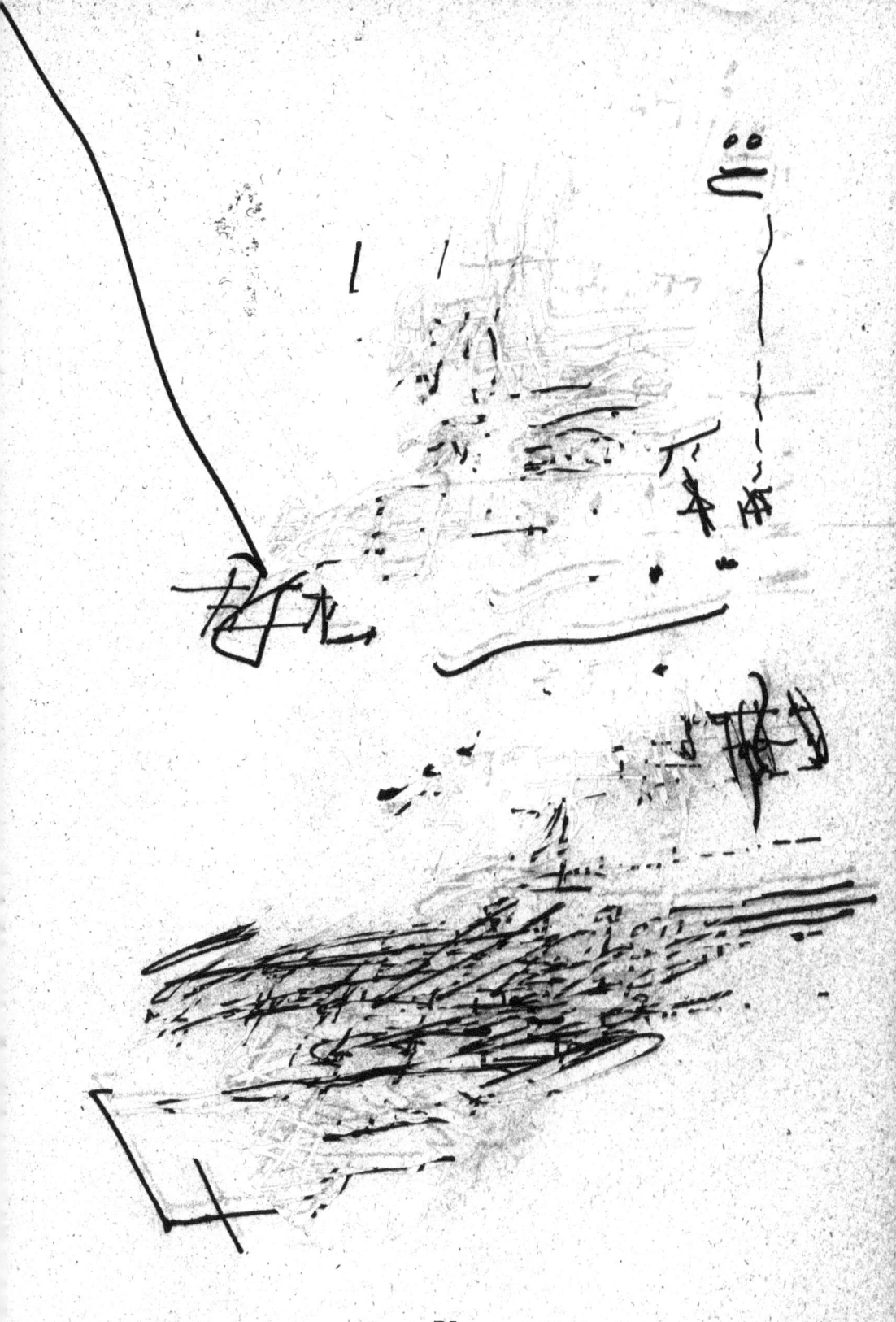

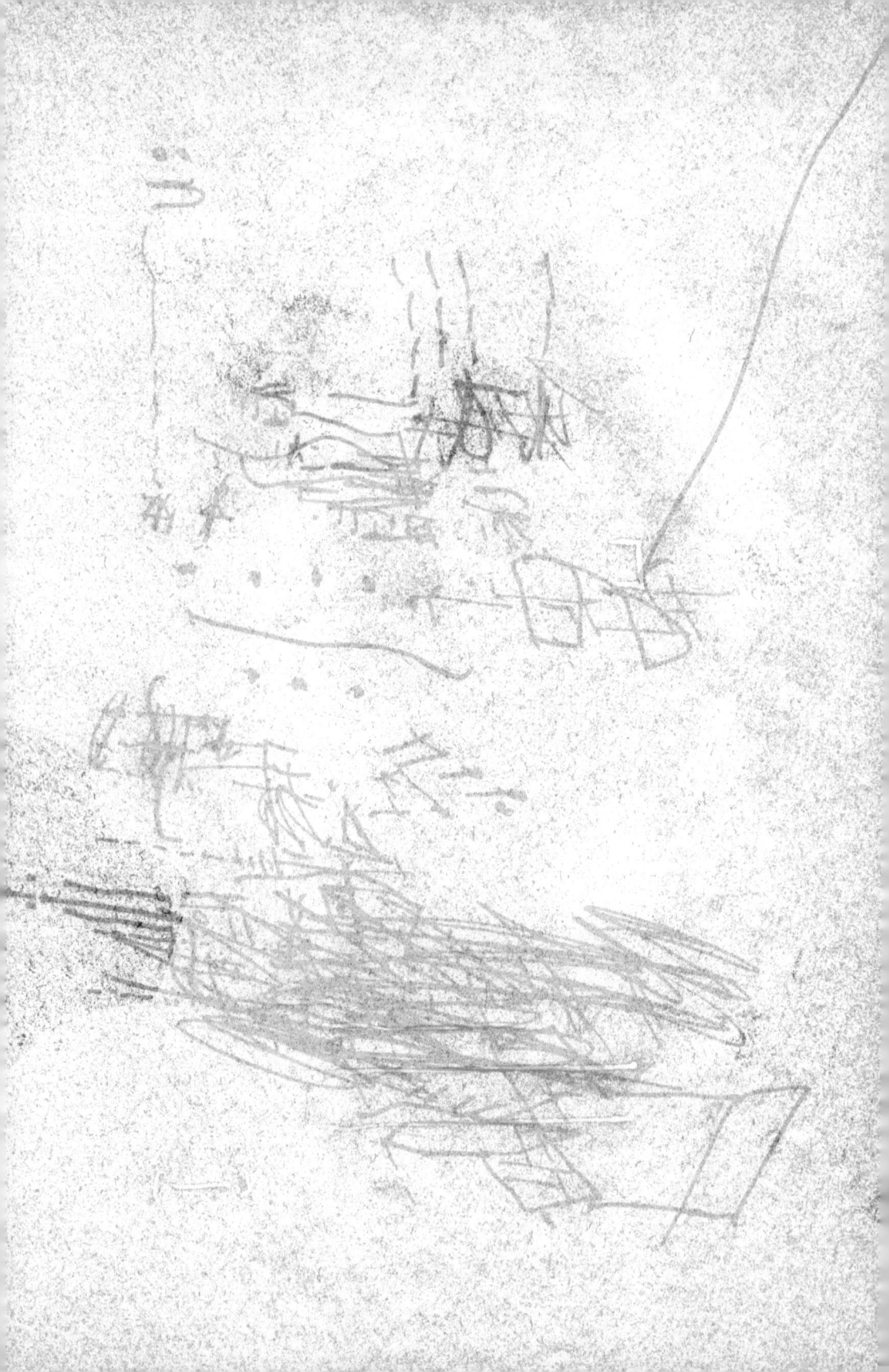

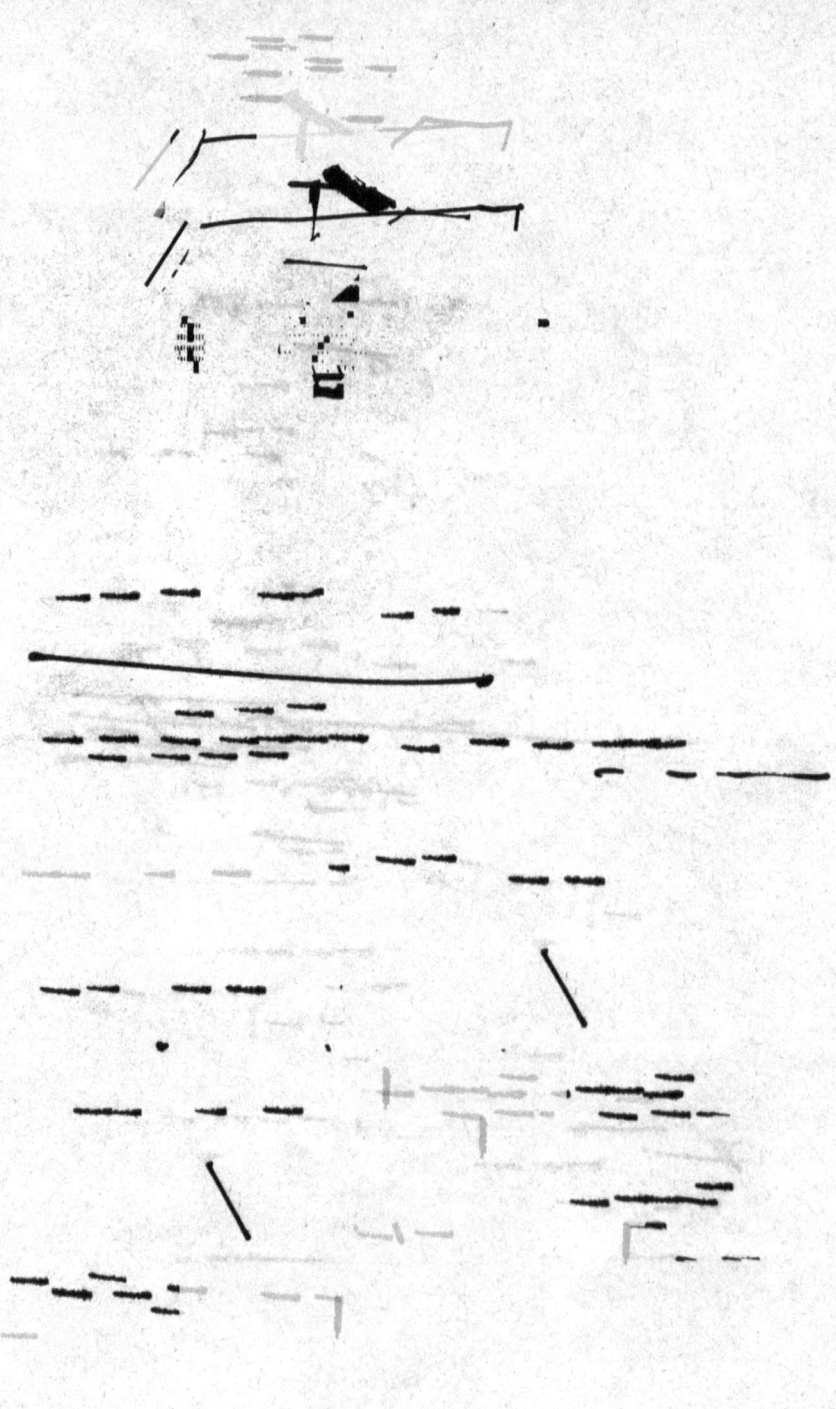

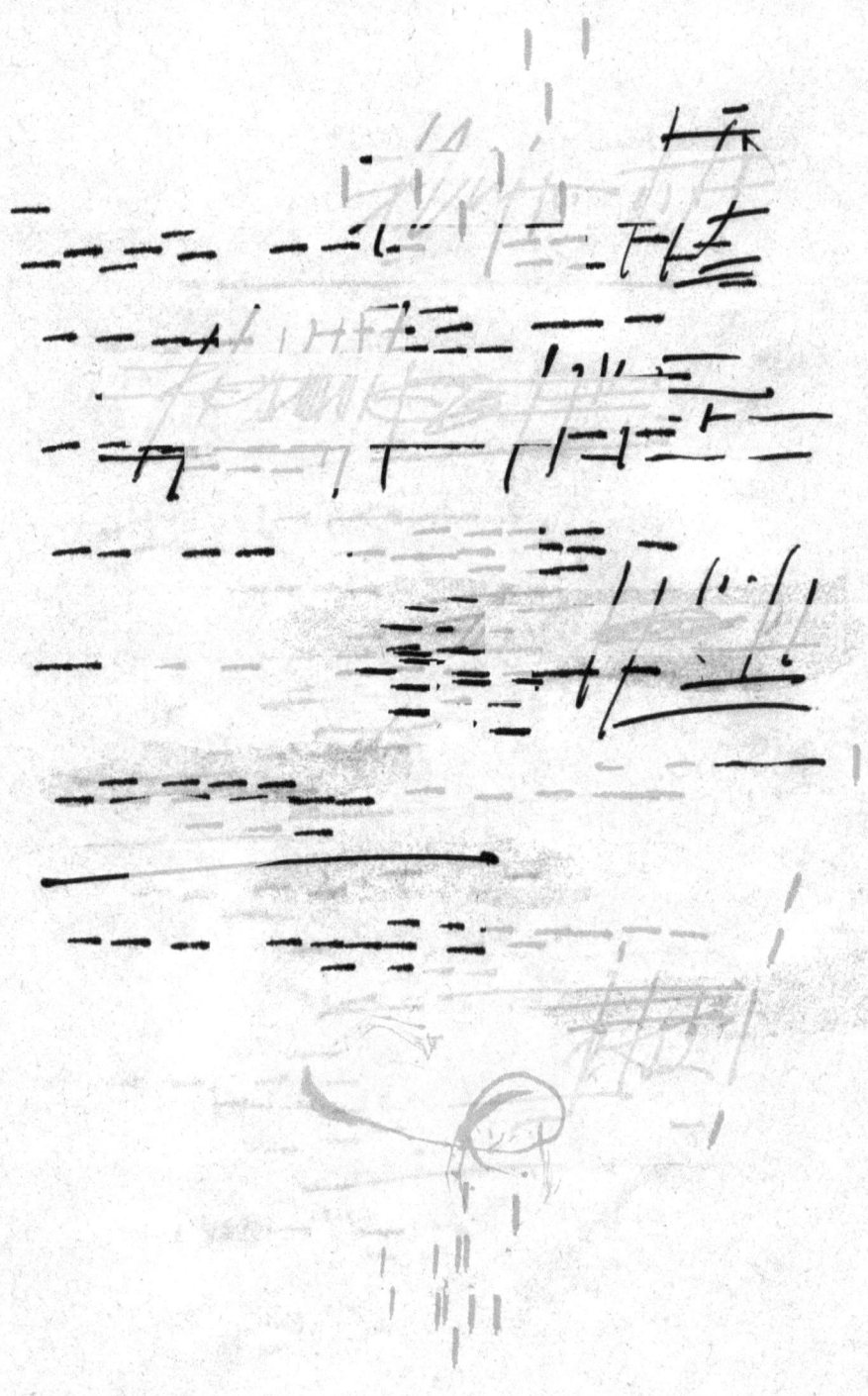

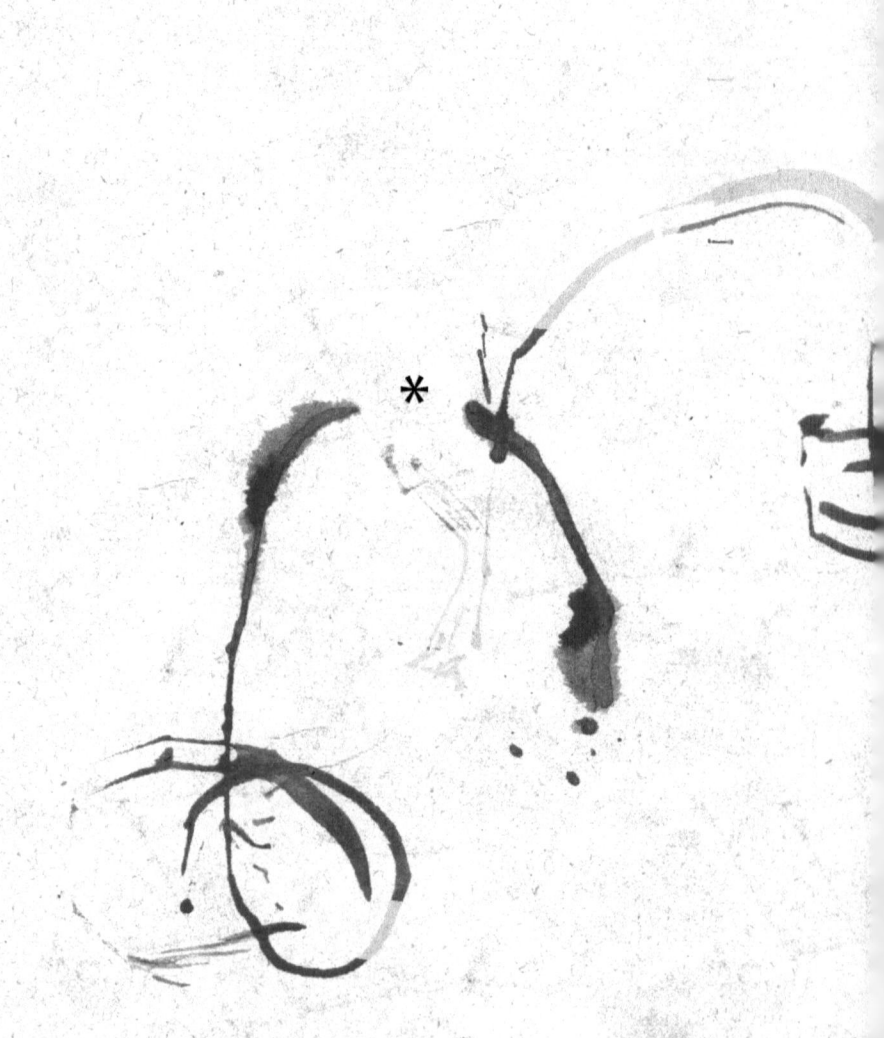

*

{ }

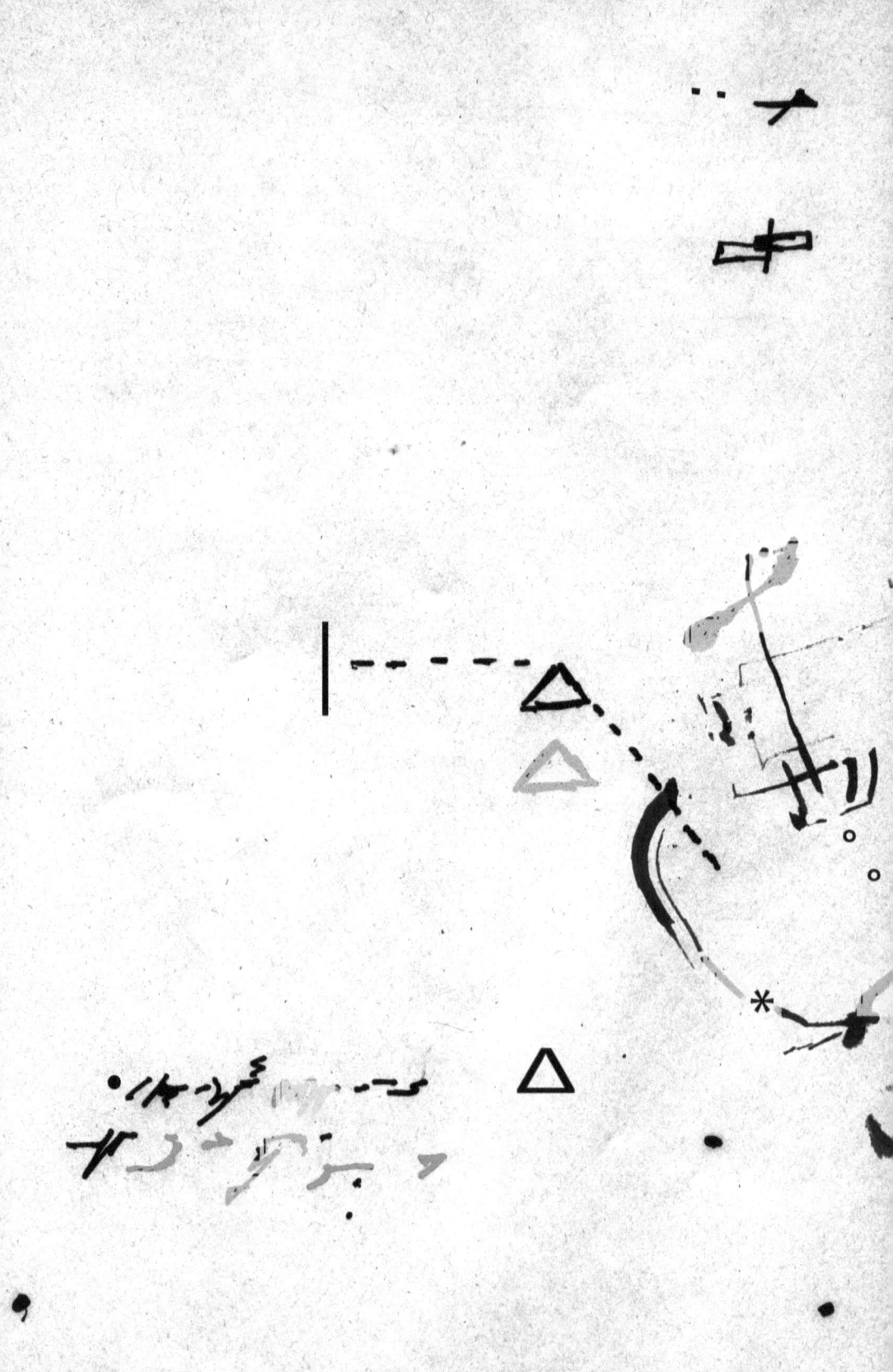

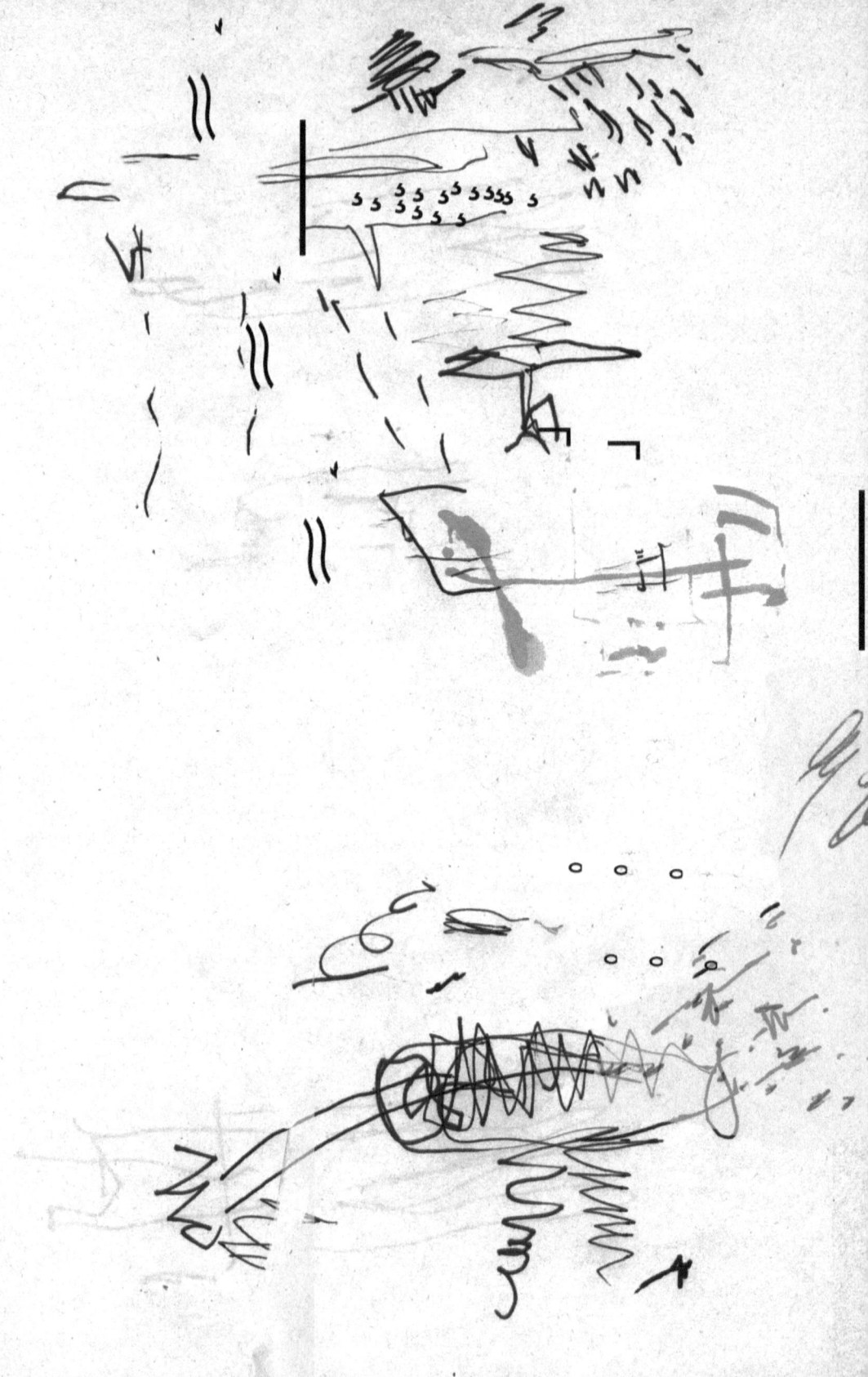

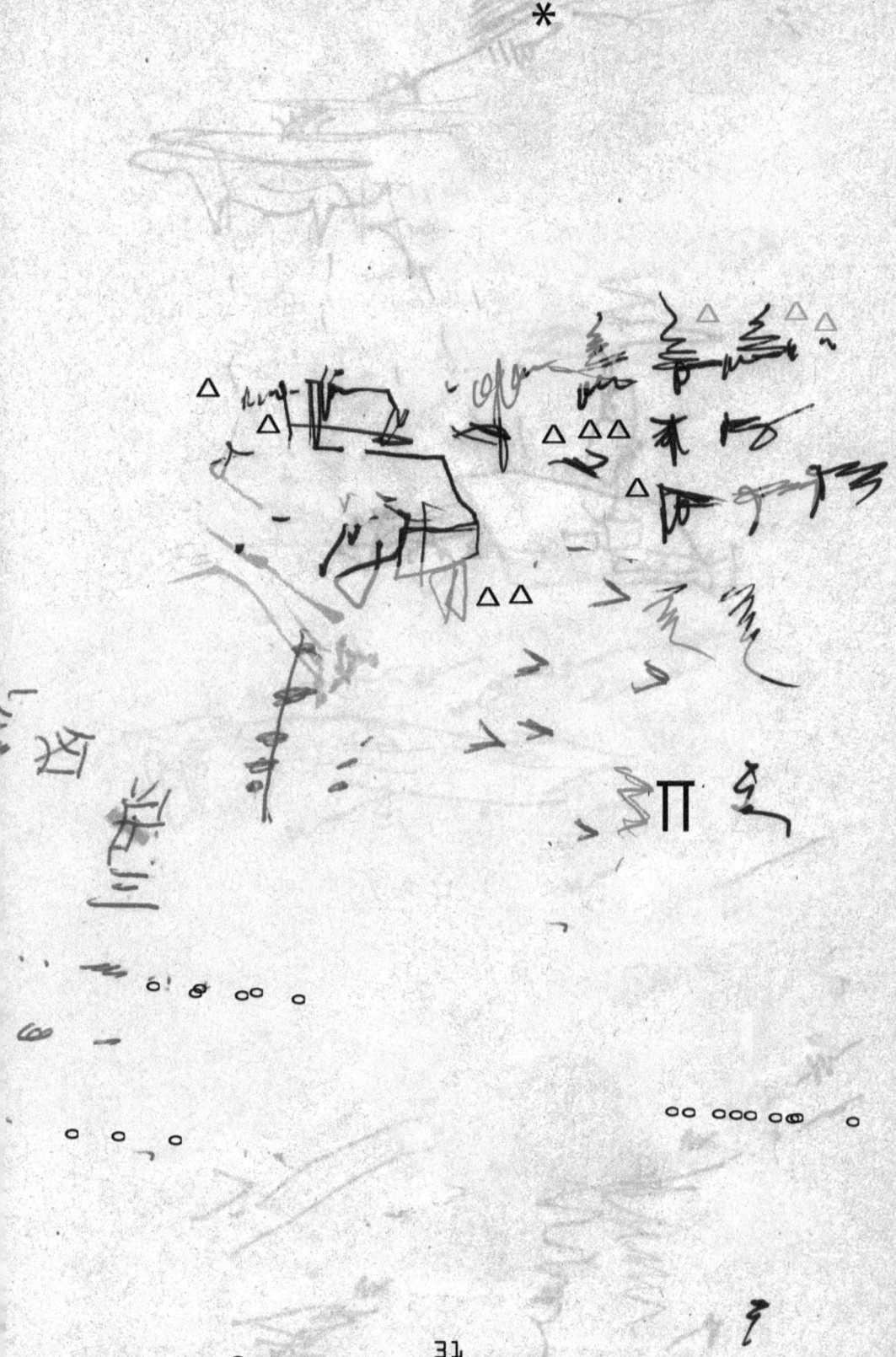

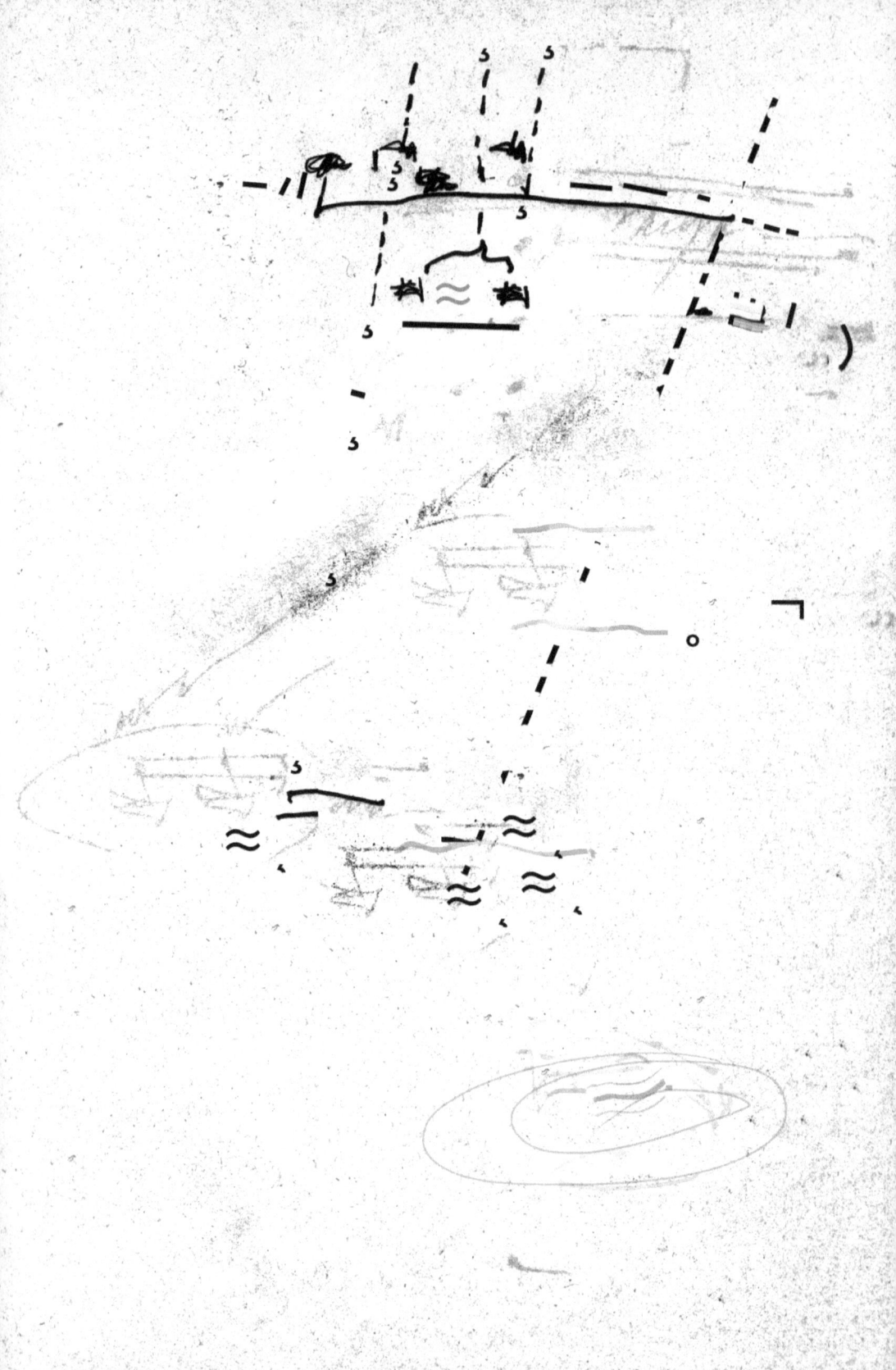

33

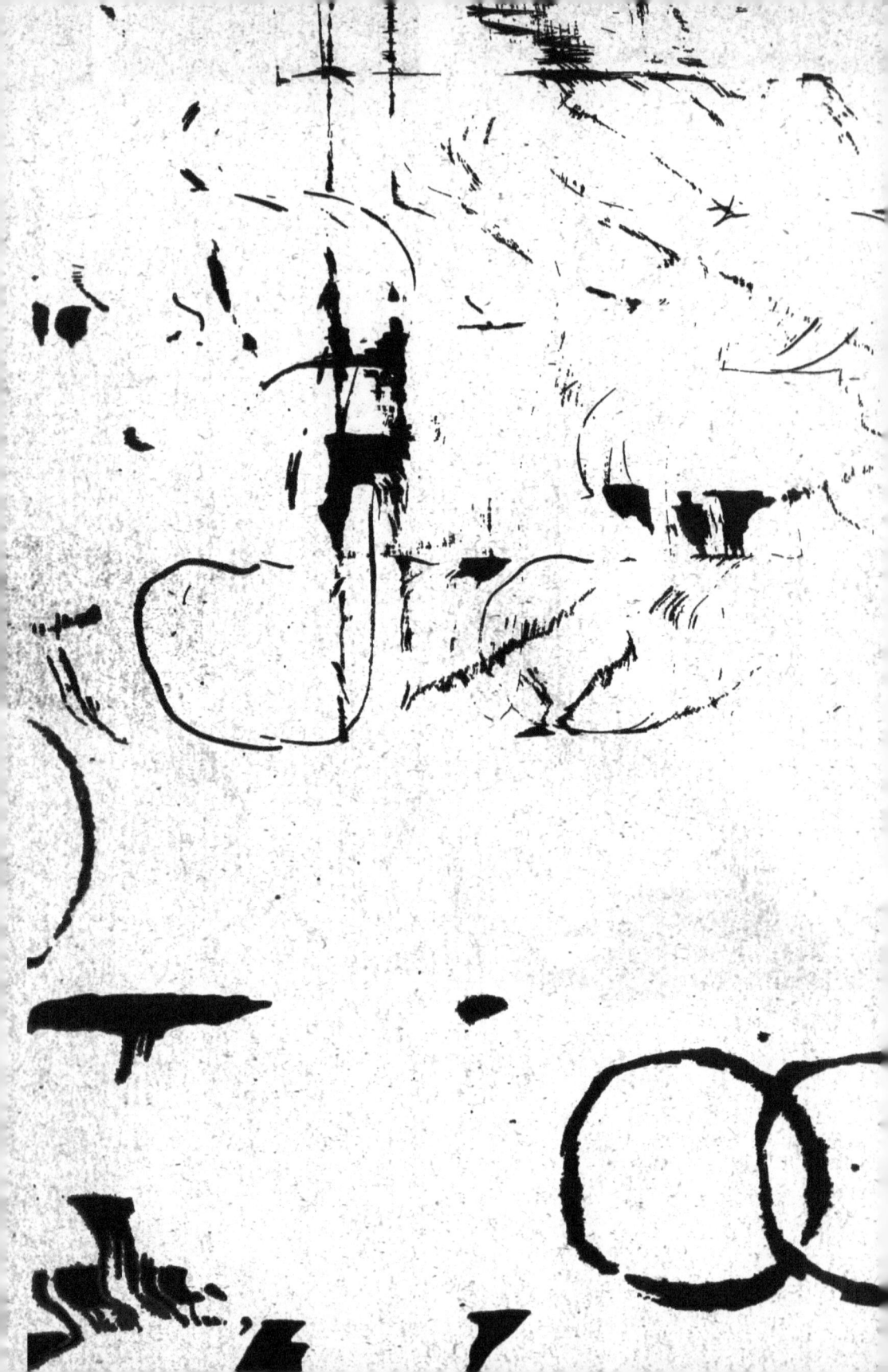

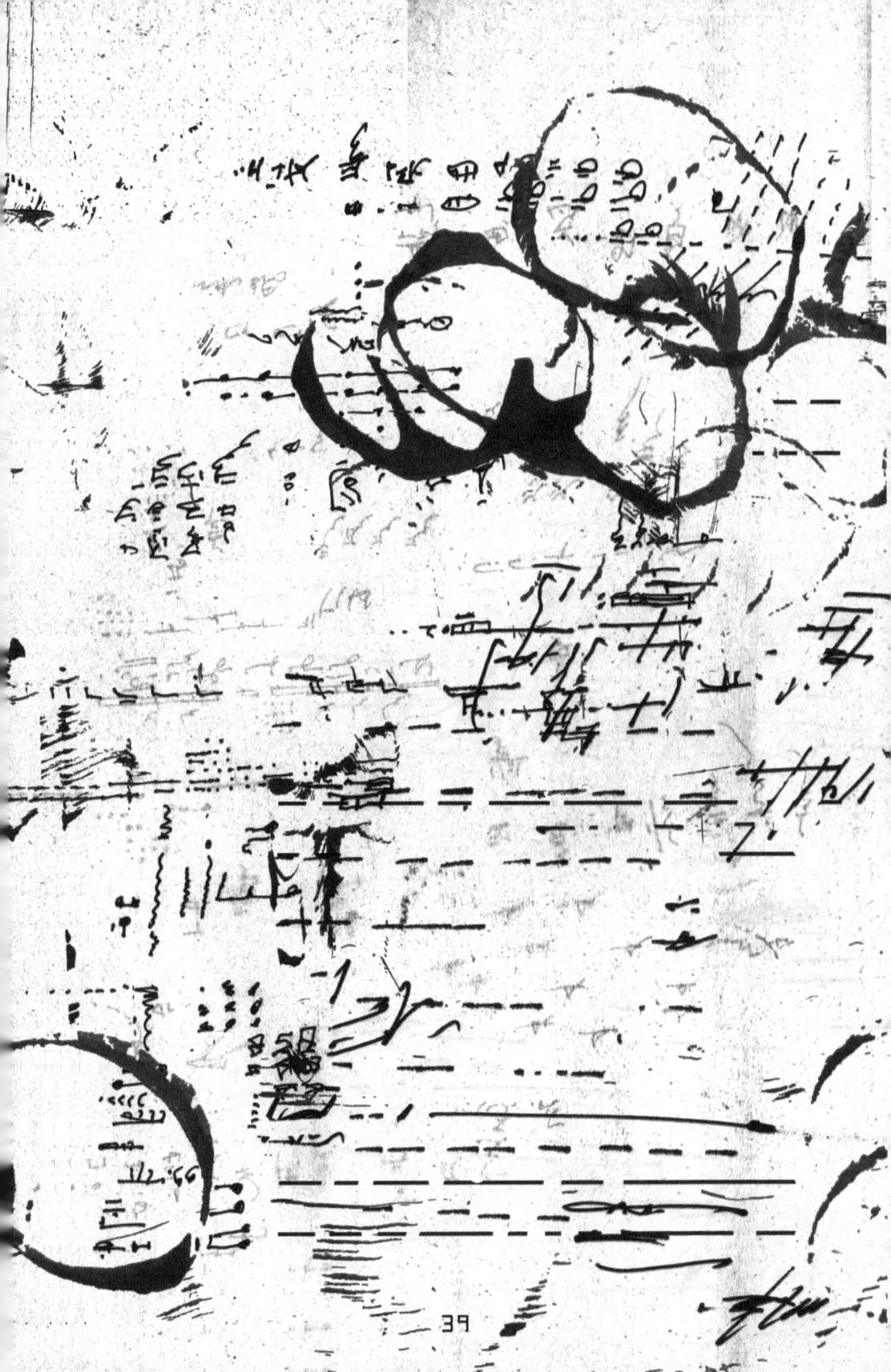

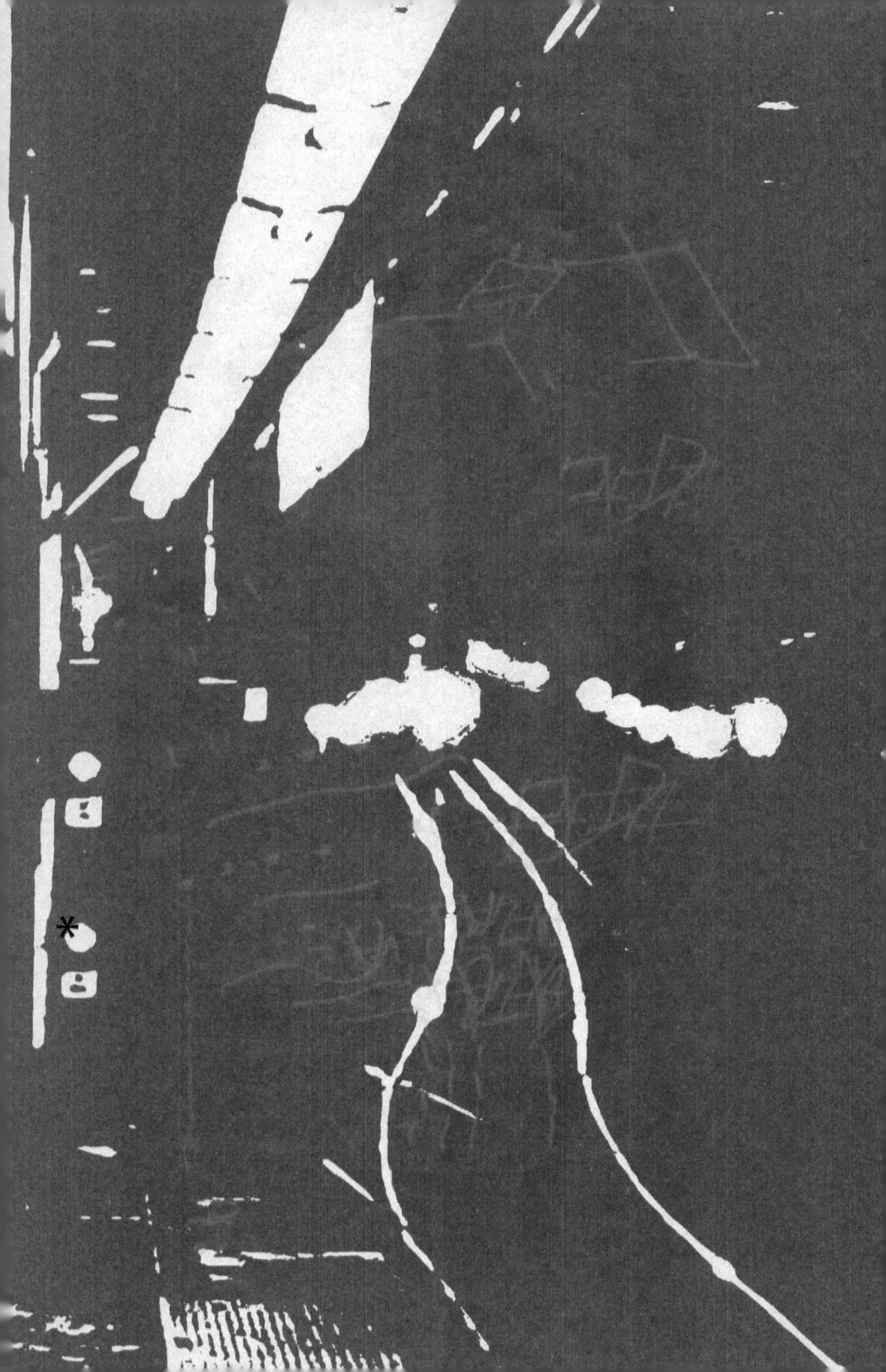

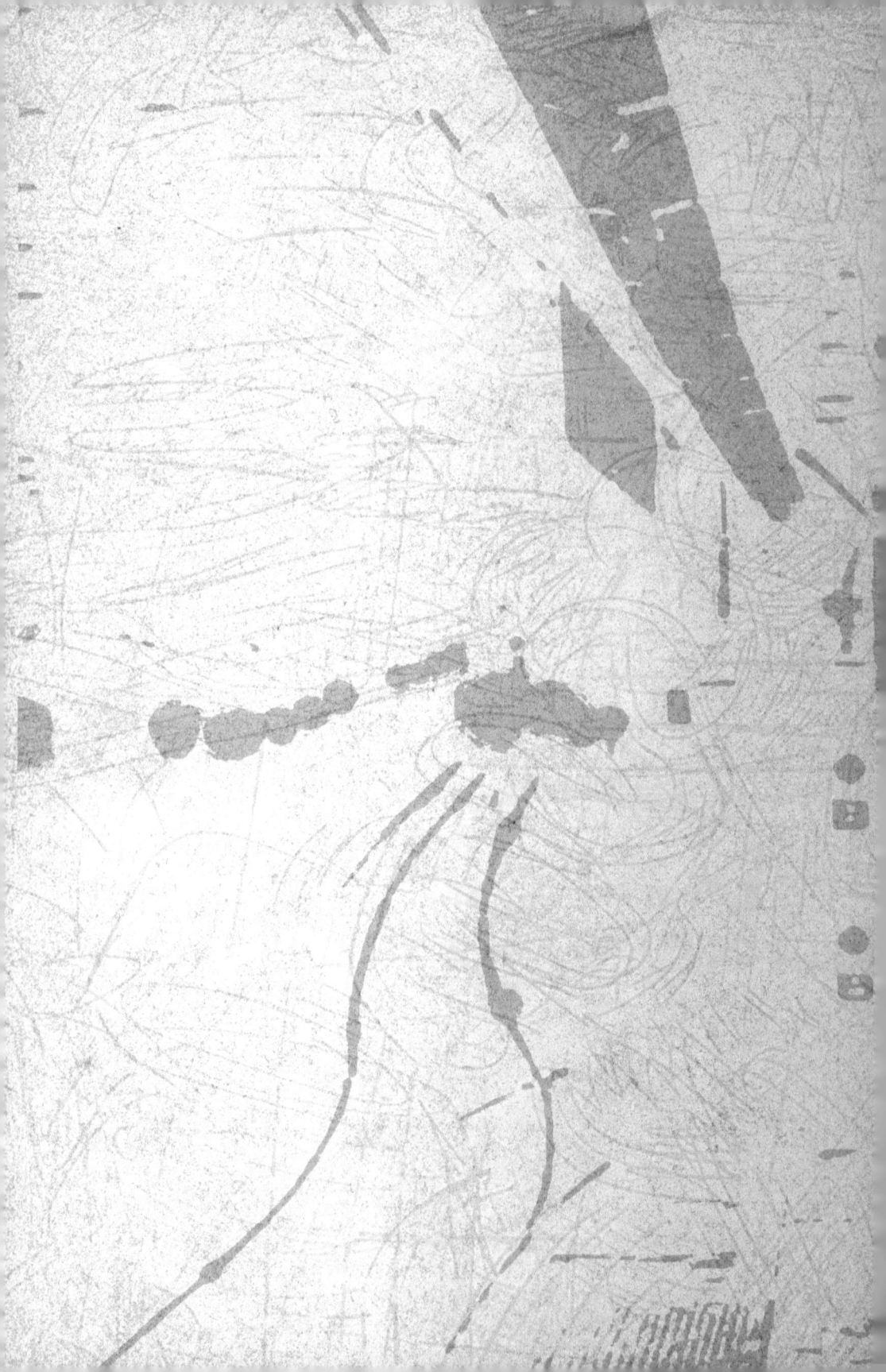

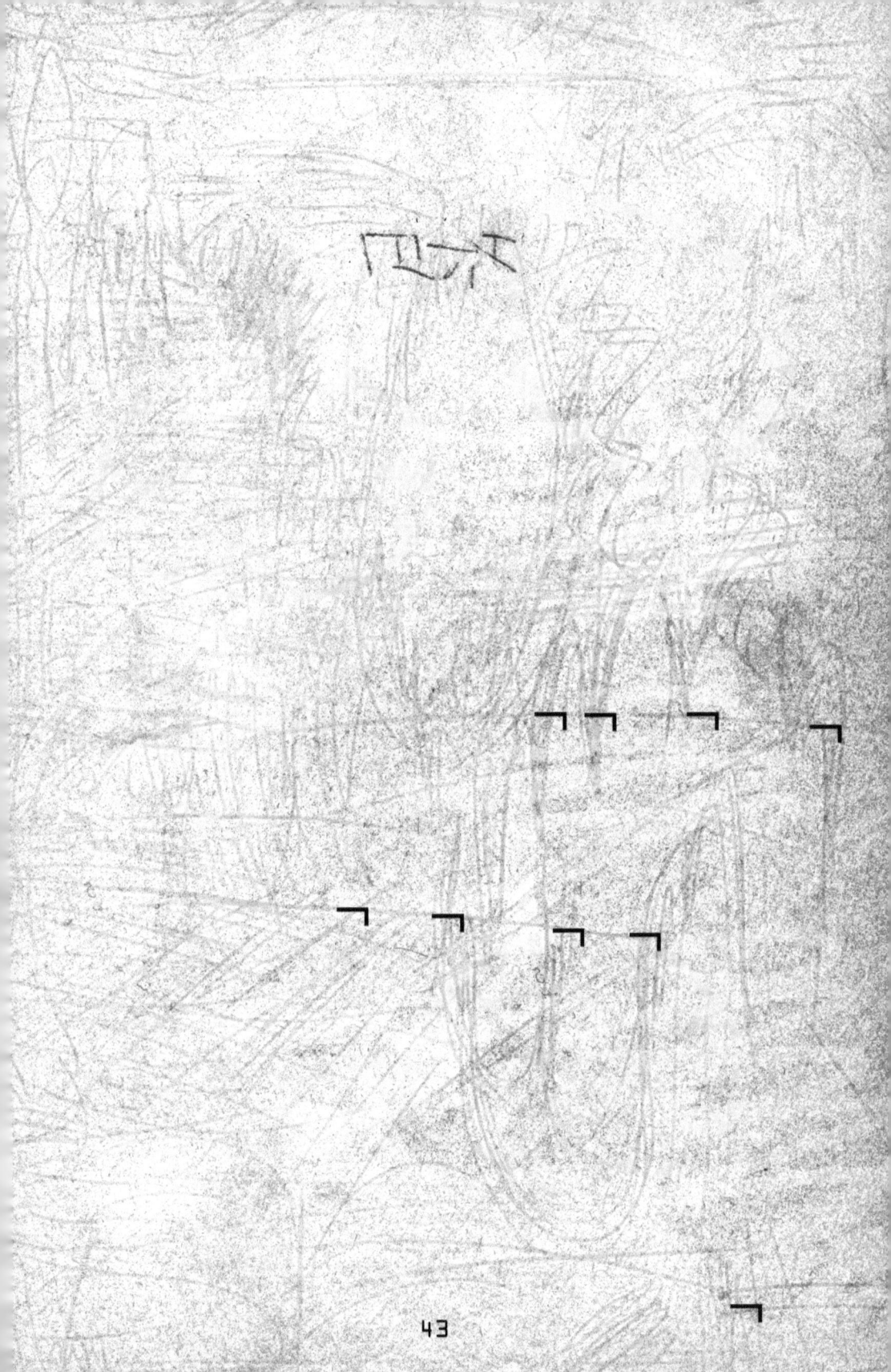

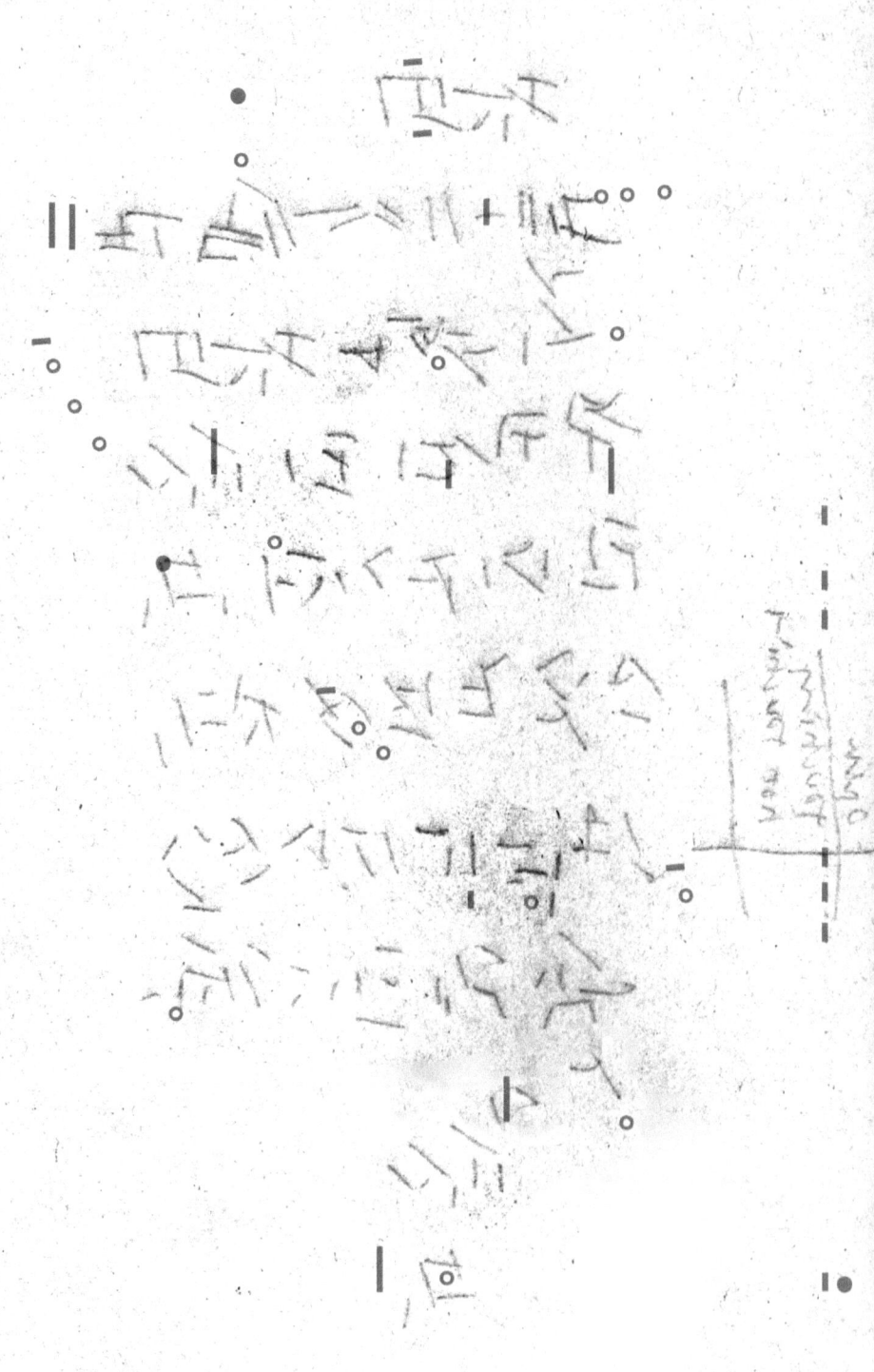

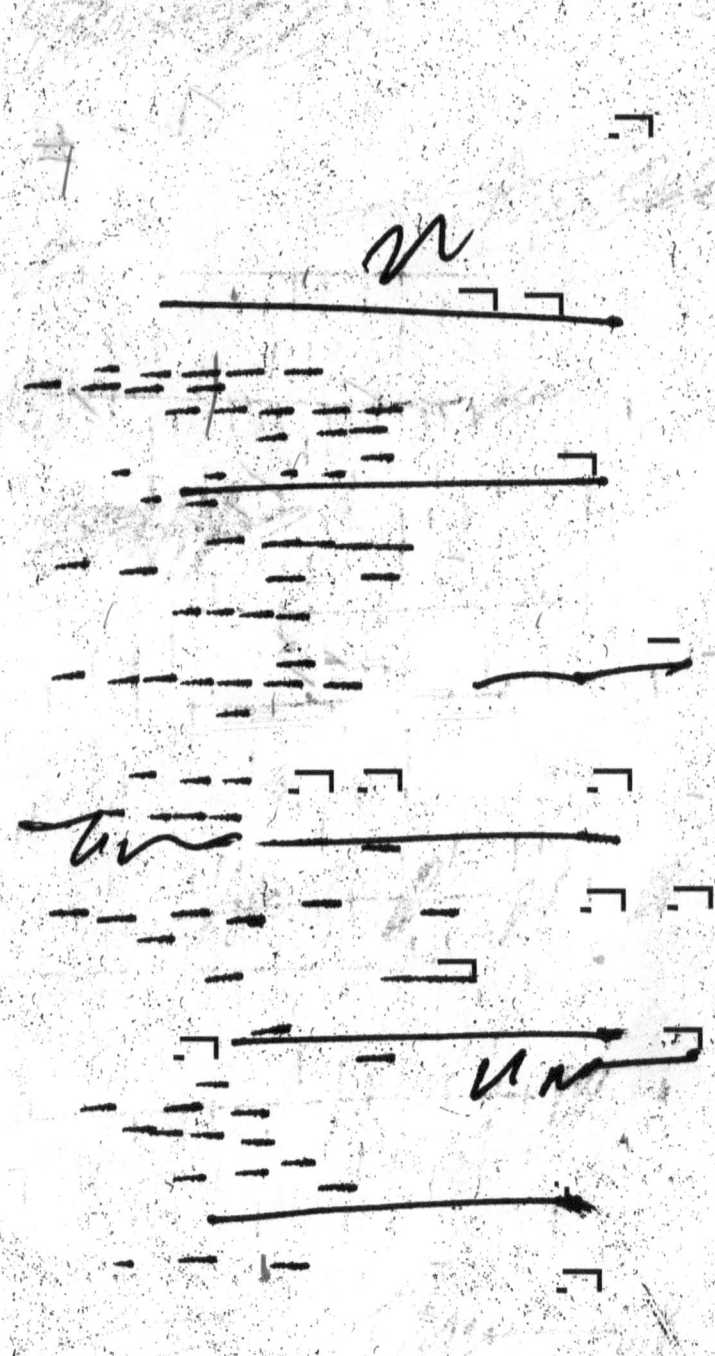

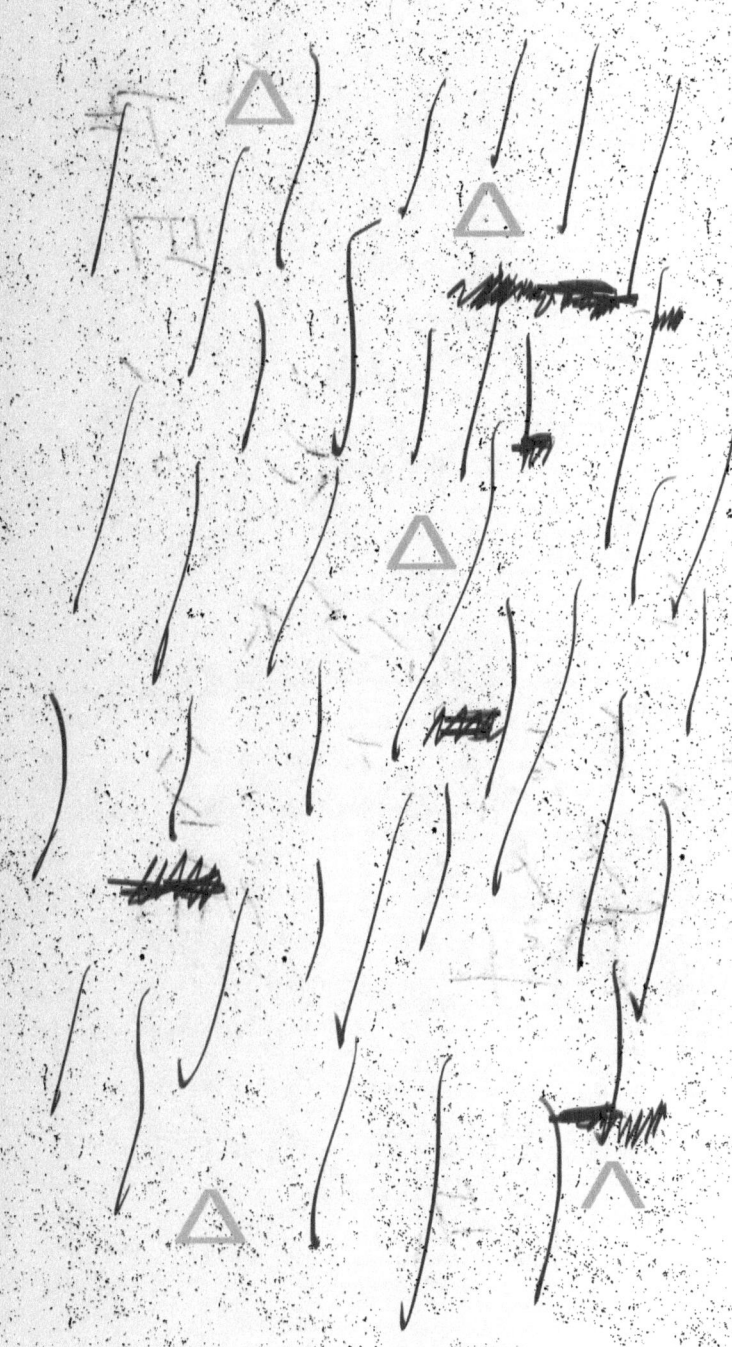

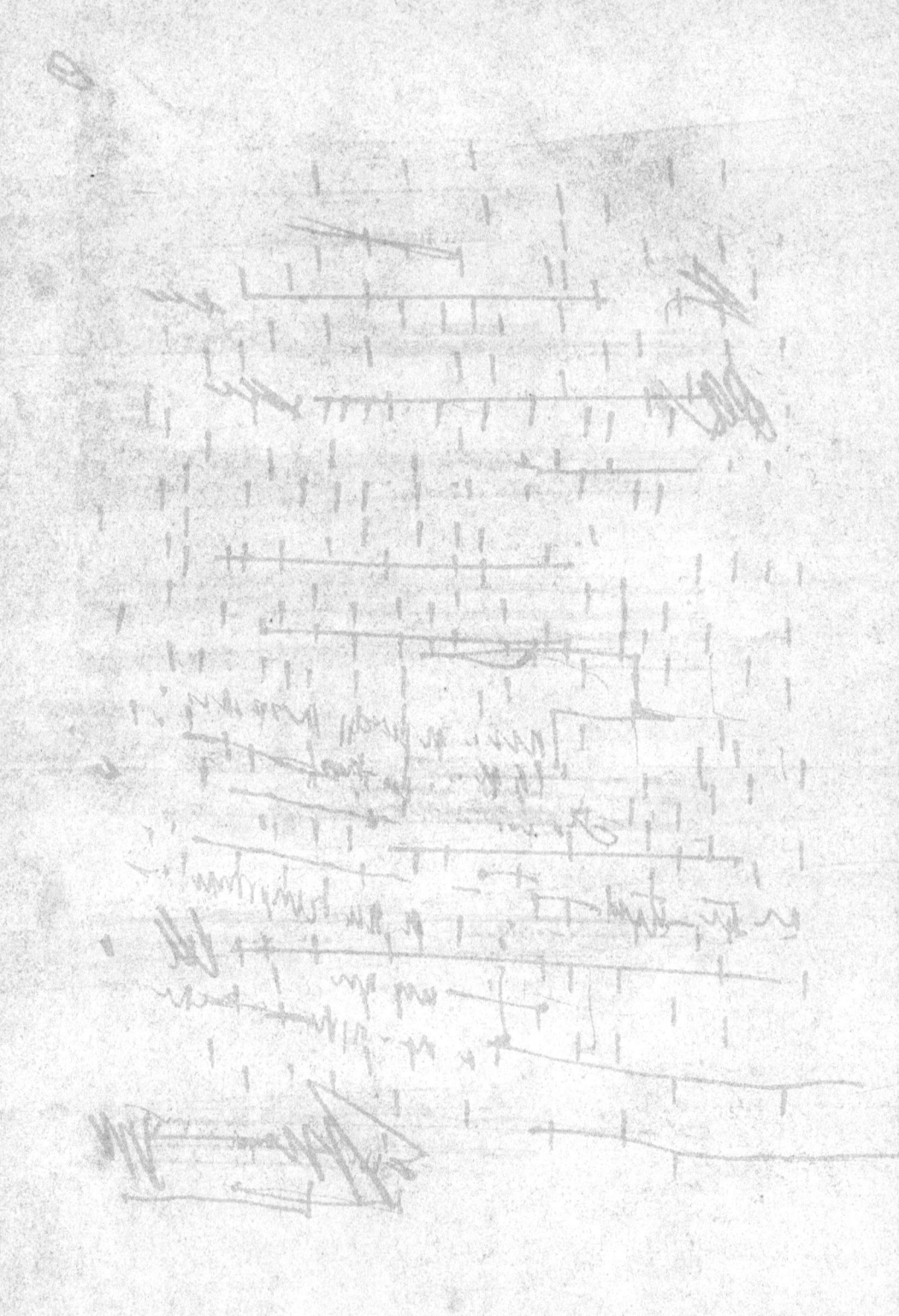

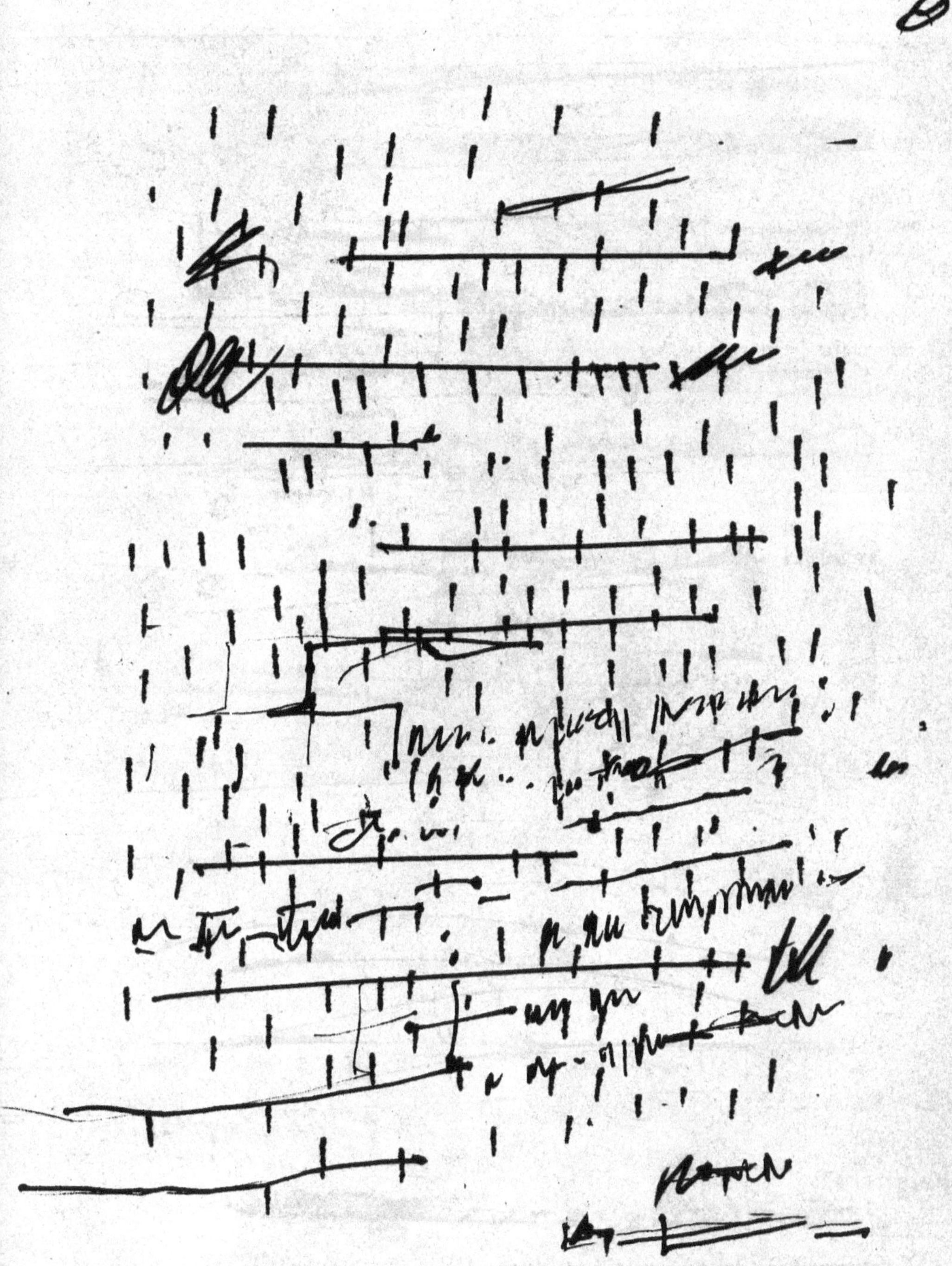

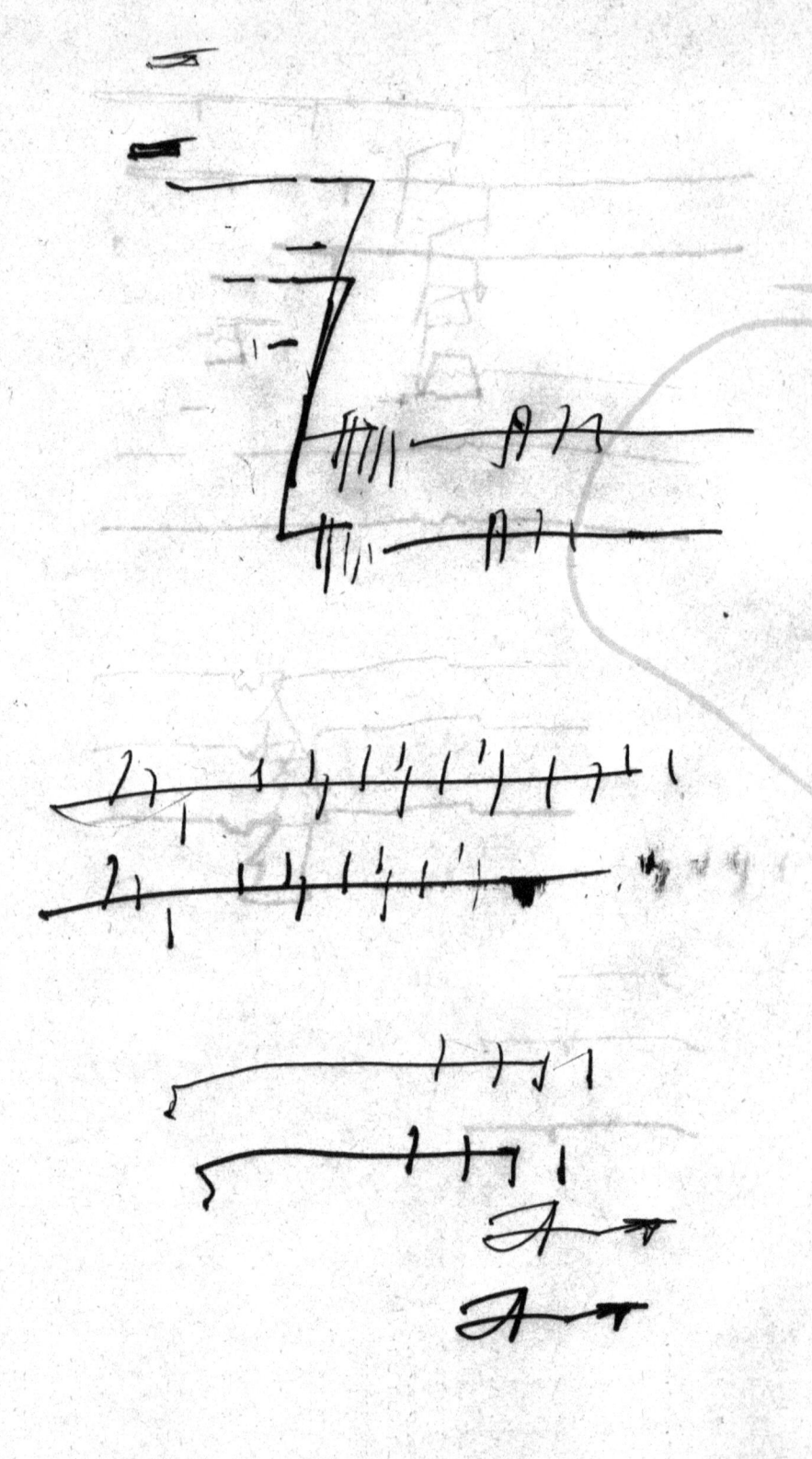

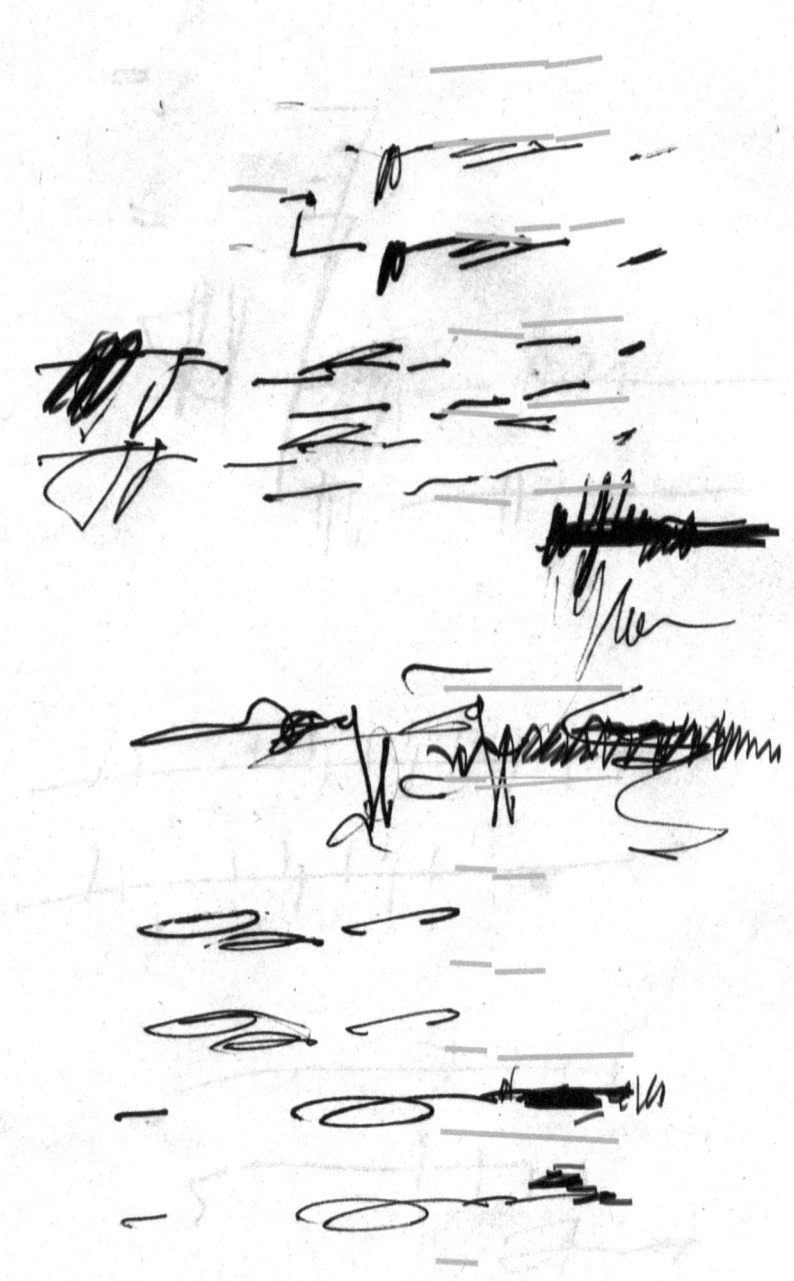

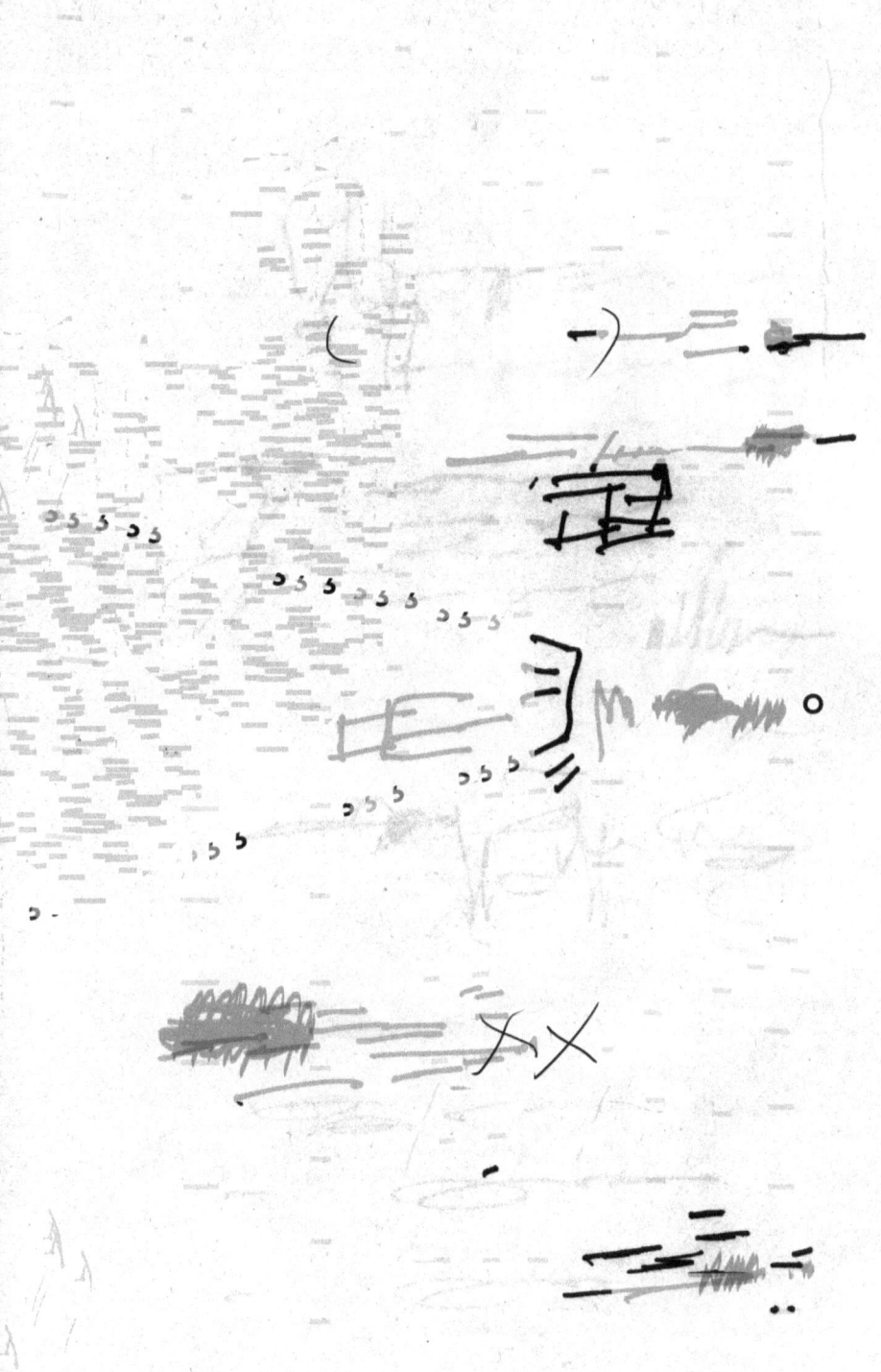

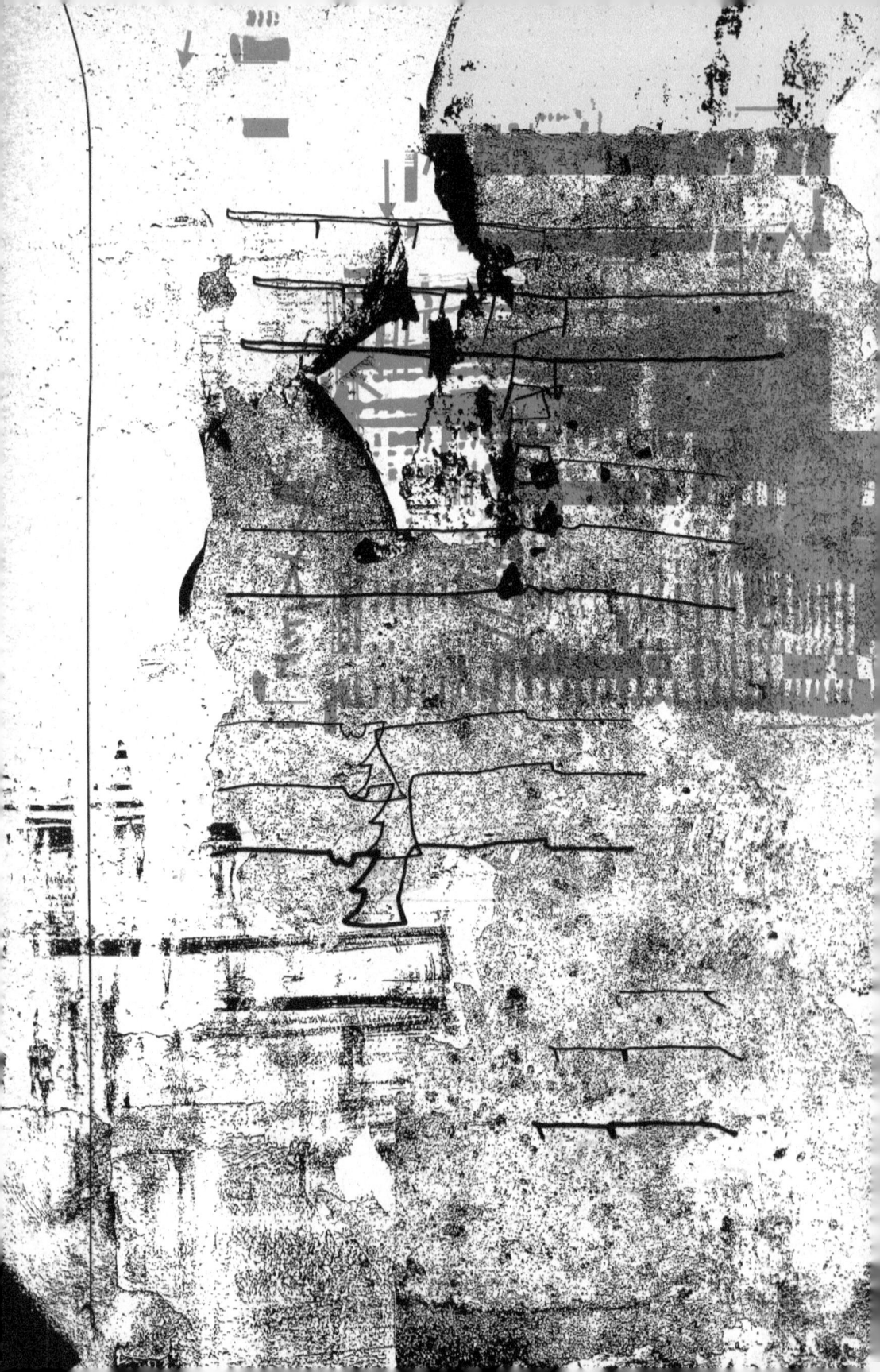

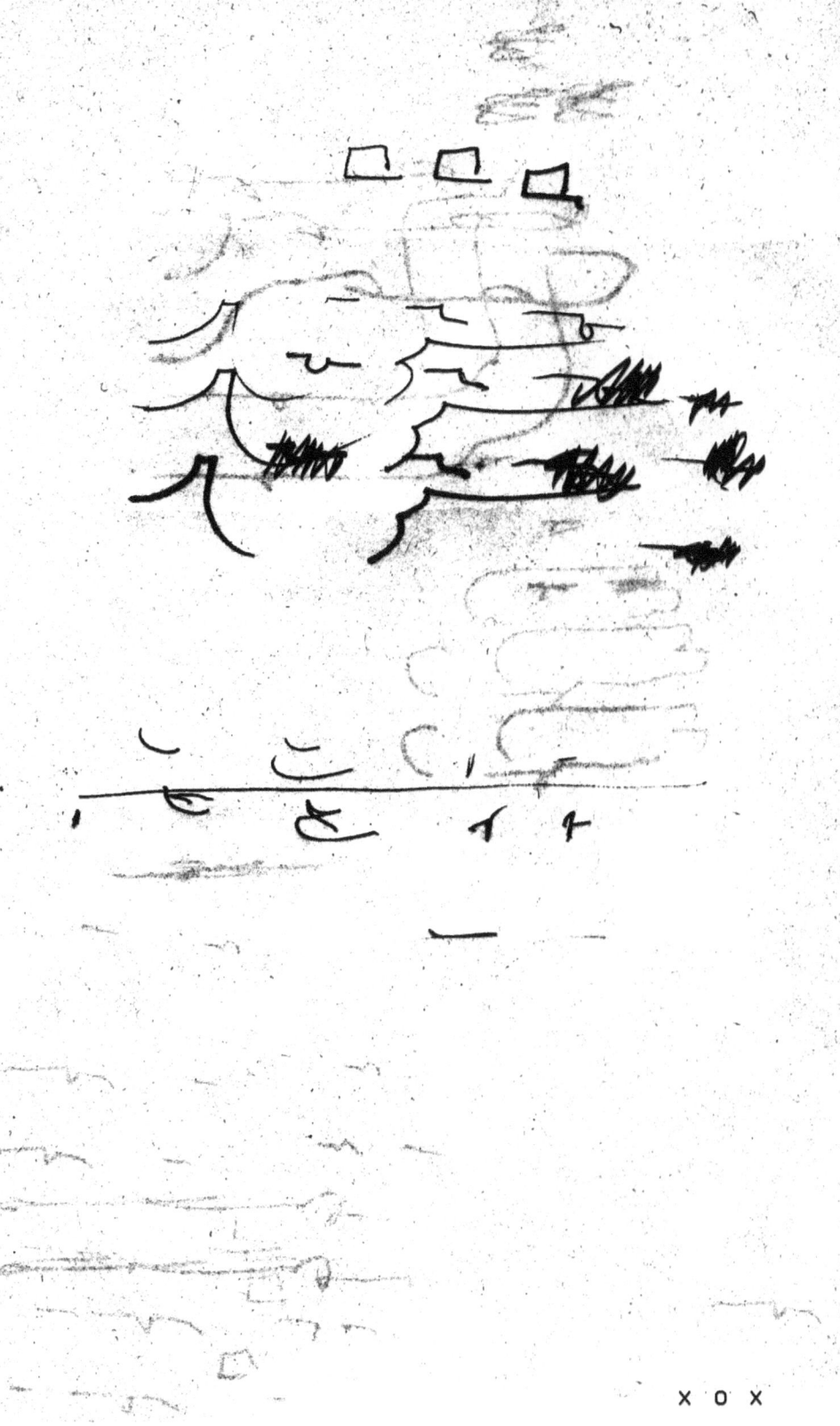

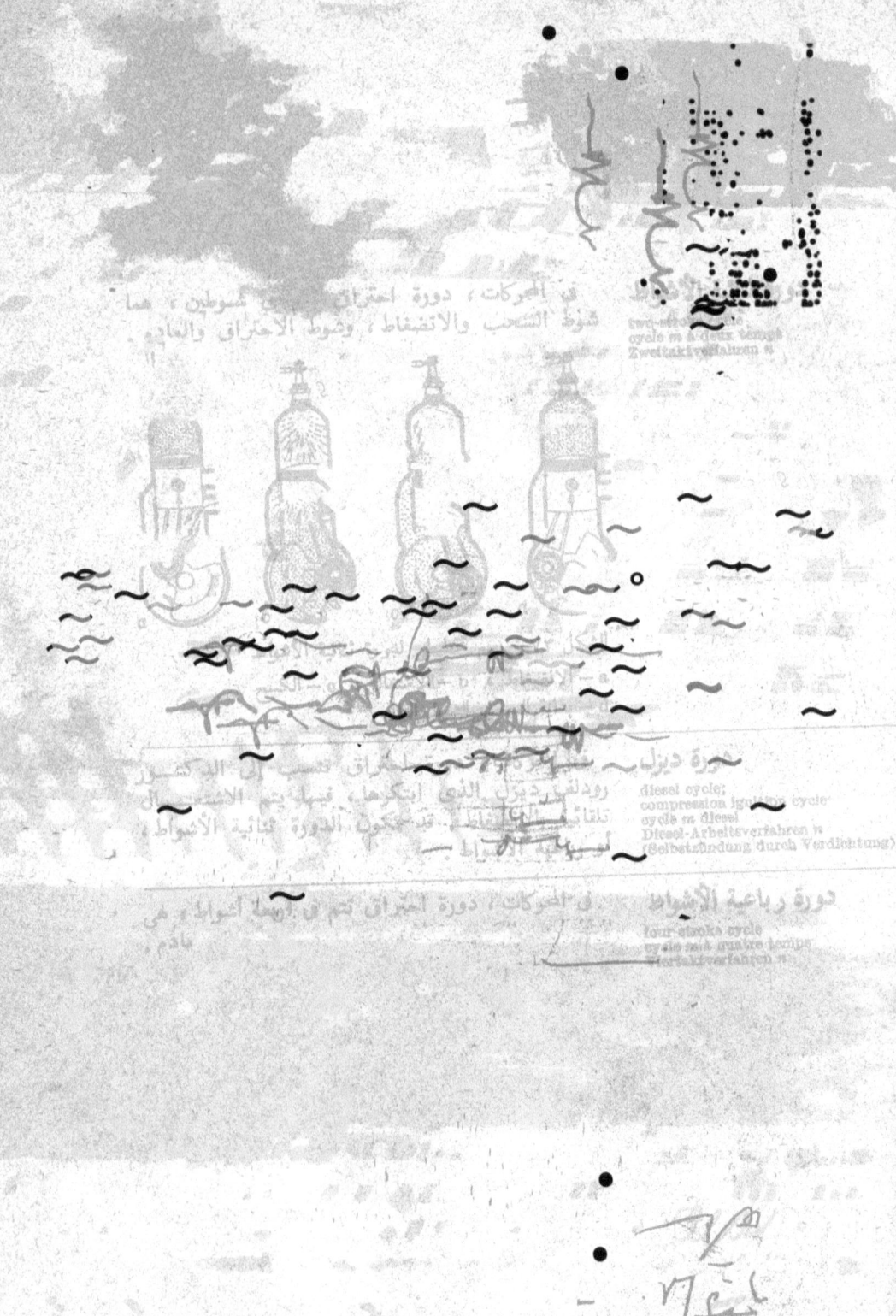

من الحركات؛ دورة احتراق شوطين ، هما
شوط السحب والانضغاط، وشوط الاحتراق والعادم

two-stroke cycle
cycle m à deux temps
Zweitaktverfahren n

دورة ديزل
diesel cycle;
compression ignition cycle
cycle en diesel
Diesel-Arbeitsverfahren n
(Selbstzündung durch Verdichtung)

دورة رباعية الأشواط في المحركات؛ دورة الاحتراق تتم في أربعة أشواط، هي
four-stroke cycle
cycle met quatre temps
Viertaktverfahren n

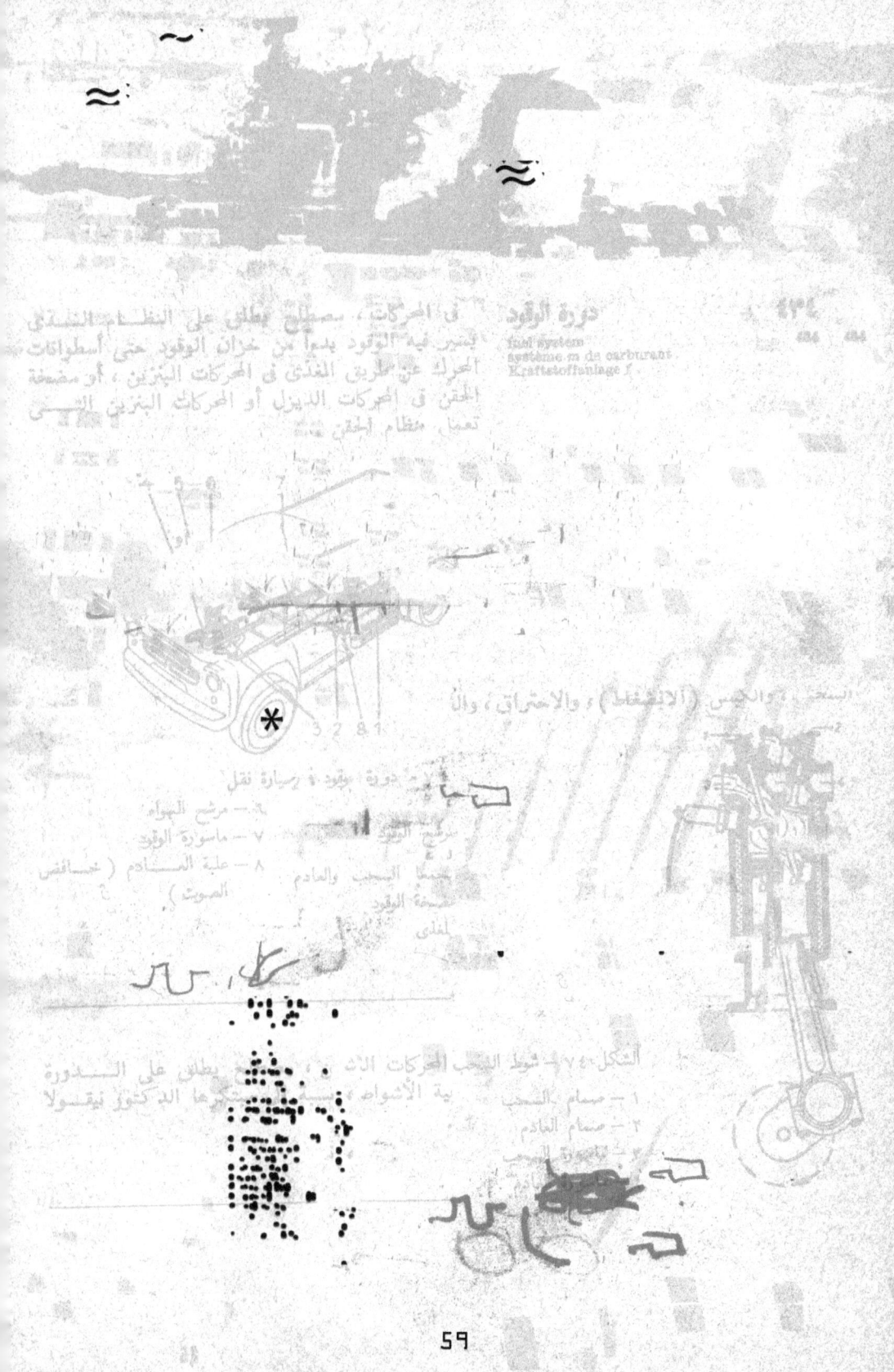

دورة الوقود
fuel system
système m da carburant.
Kraftstoffanlage f.

فى المحركات ، مصطلح يطلق على النظام النفطى يمرر فيه الوقود بدءا من خزان الوقود حتى أسطوانات المحرك عن طريق المغذى فى المحركات البنزين ، أو مضخة الحقن فى محركات الديزل أو المحركات البنزين التى تعمل بنظام الحقن

السحب والكبس ( الانضغاط ) ، والاحتراق ، والا

دورة وقود ، سيارة نقل

٦ — مرشح الهواء
٧ — ماسورة الوقود
٨ — علبة المصادم ( خافض الصوت )

الشكل ٧٤ — شوط الكبس المحركات الأث ... يطلق على الدورة نية الأشواط ... ها الدكتور نيقولا

١ — صمام السحب
٢ — صمام العادم

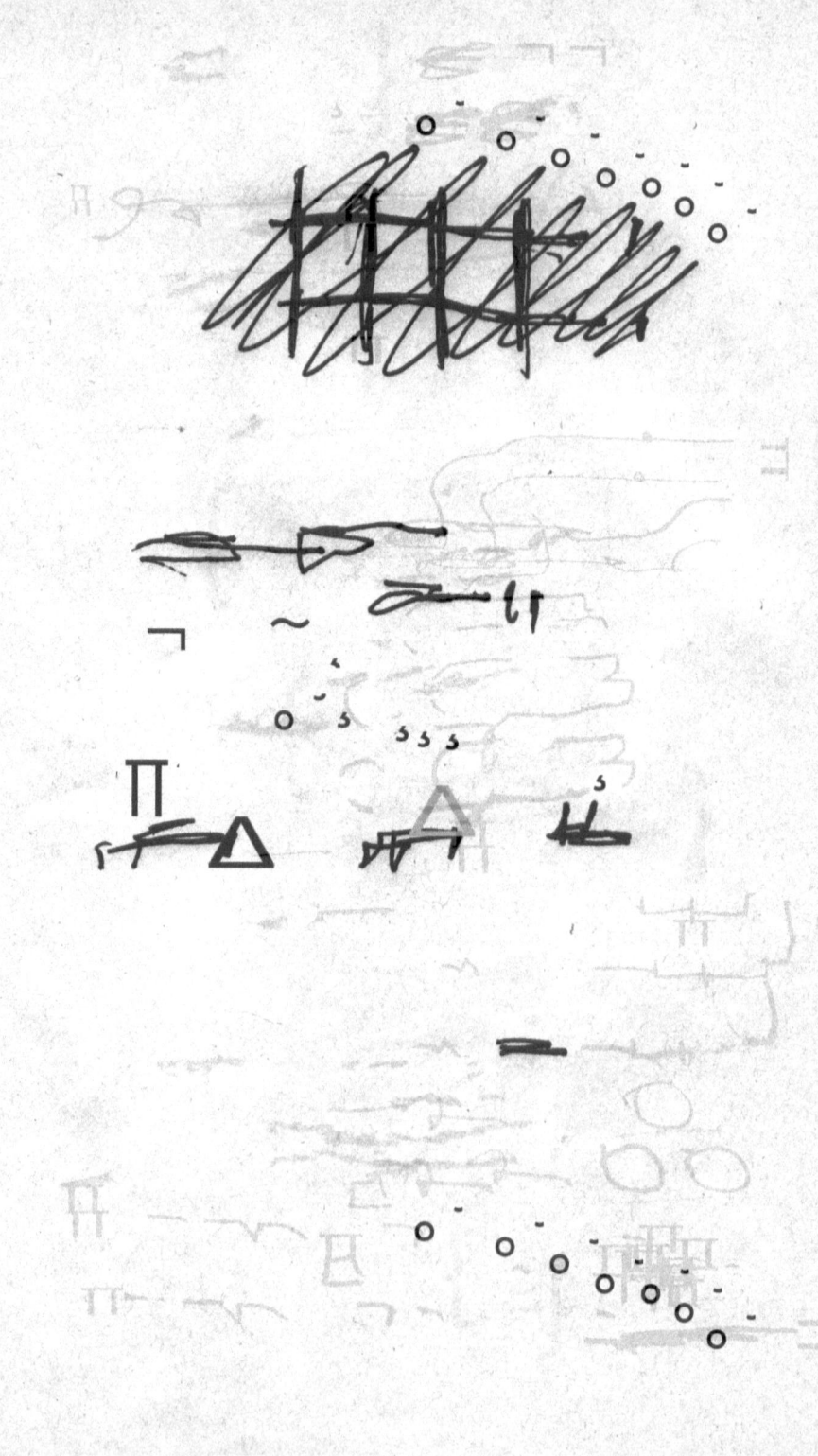

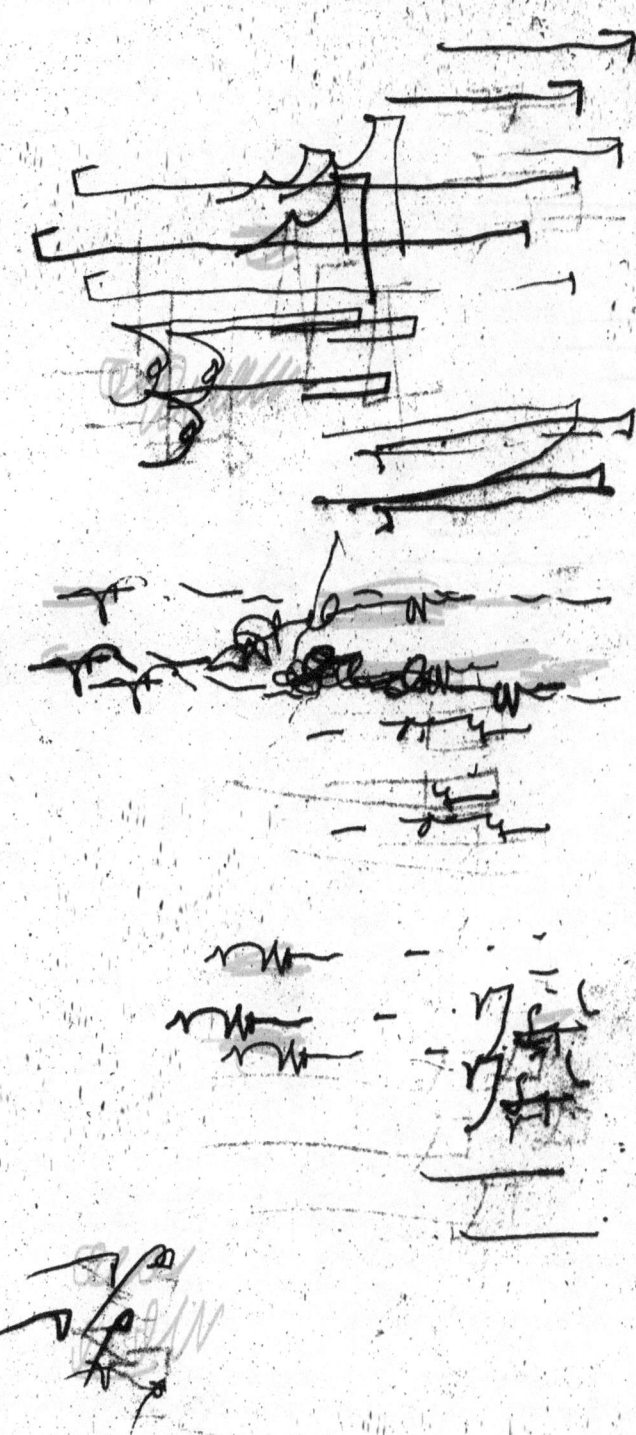

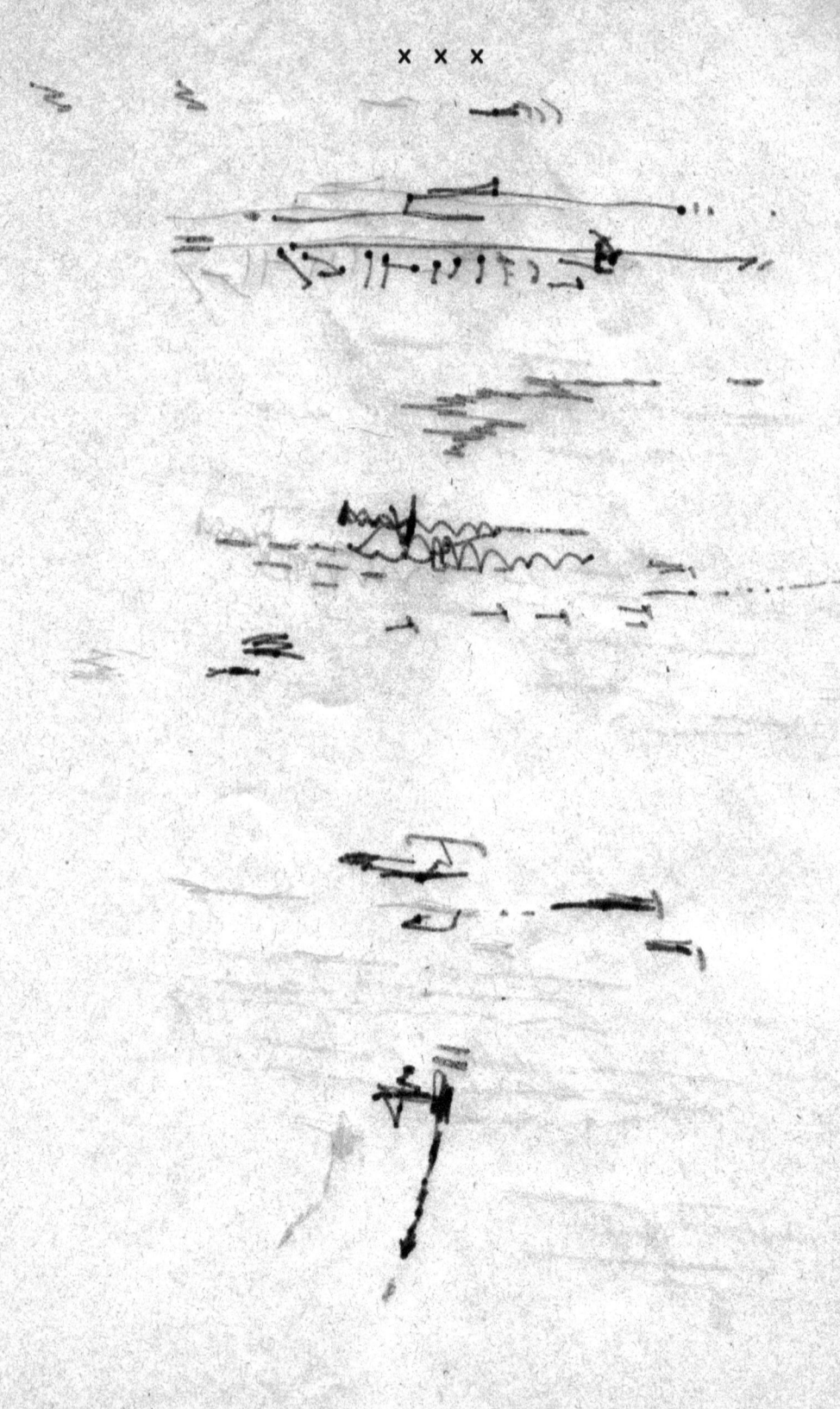

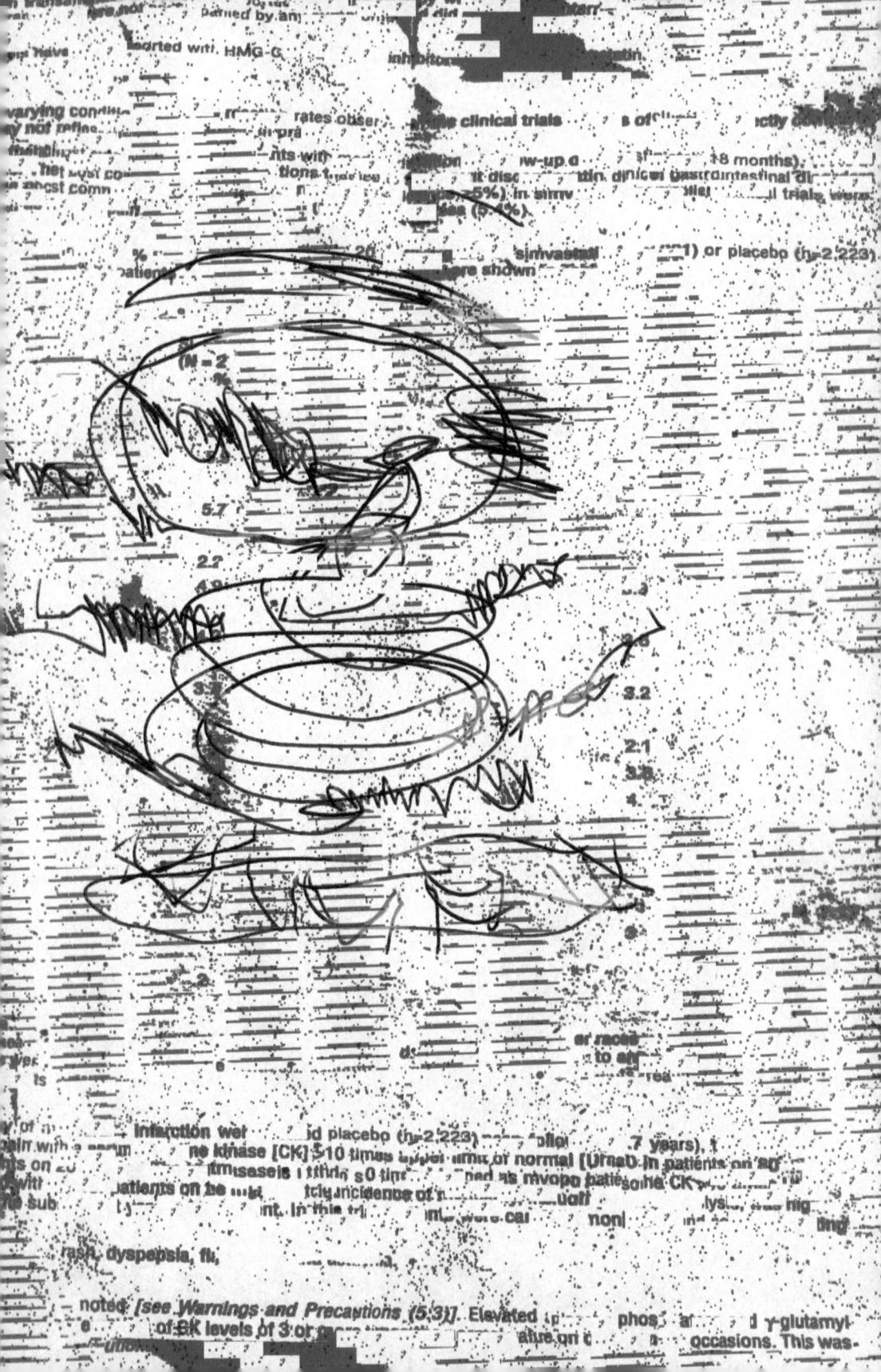

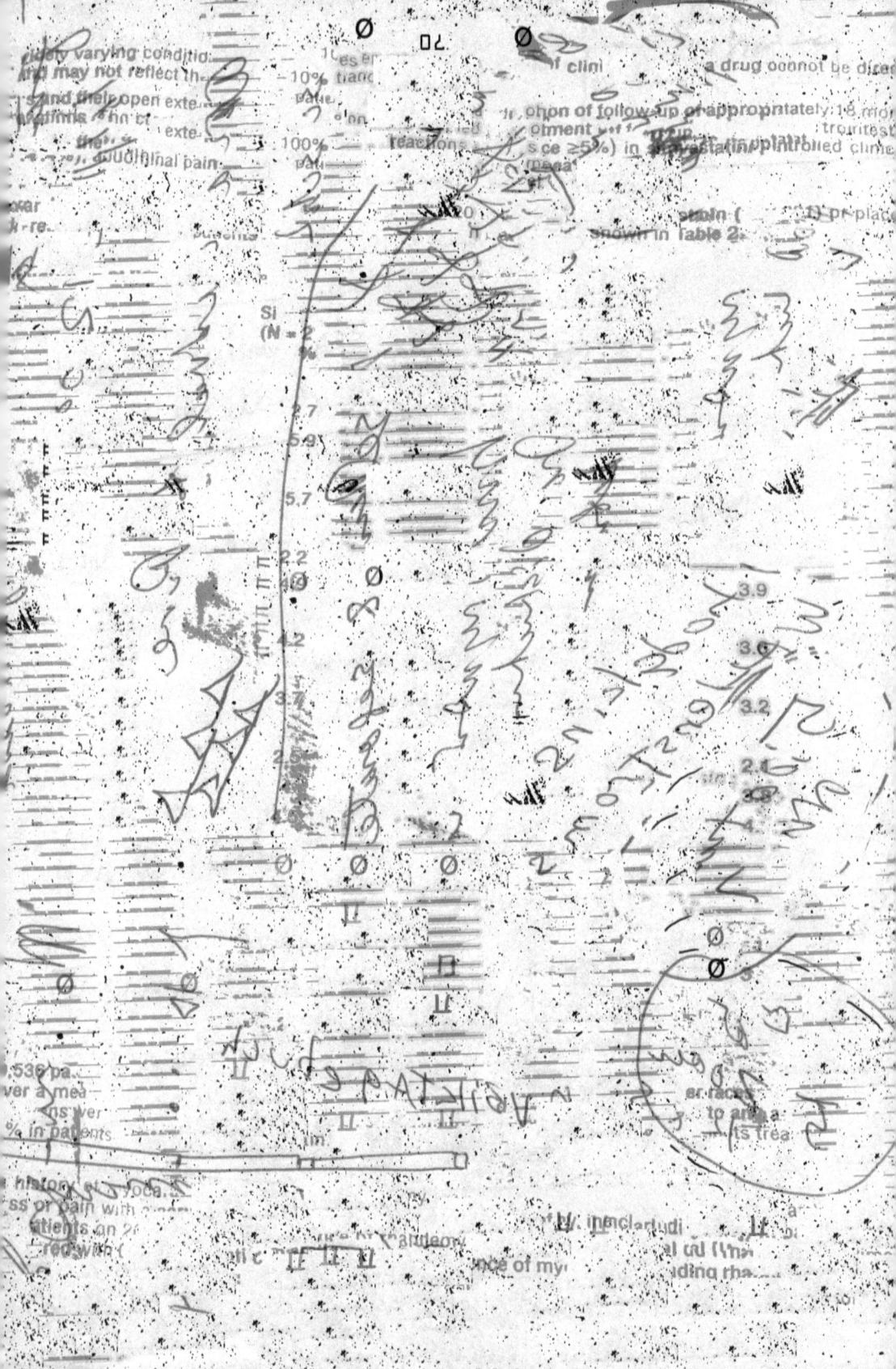

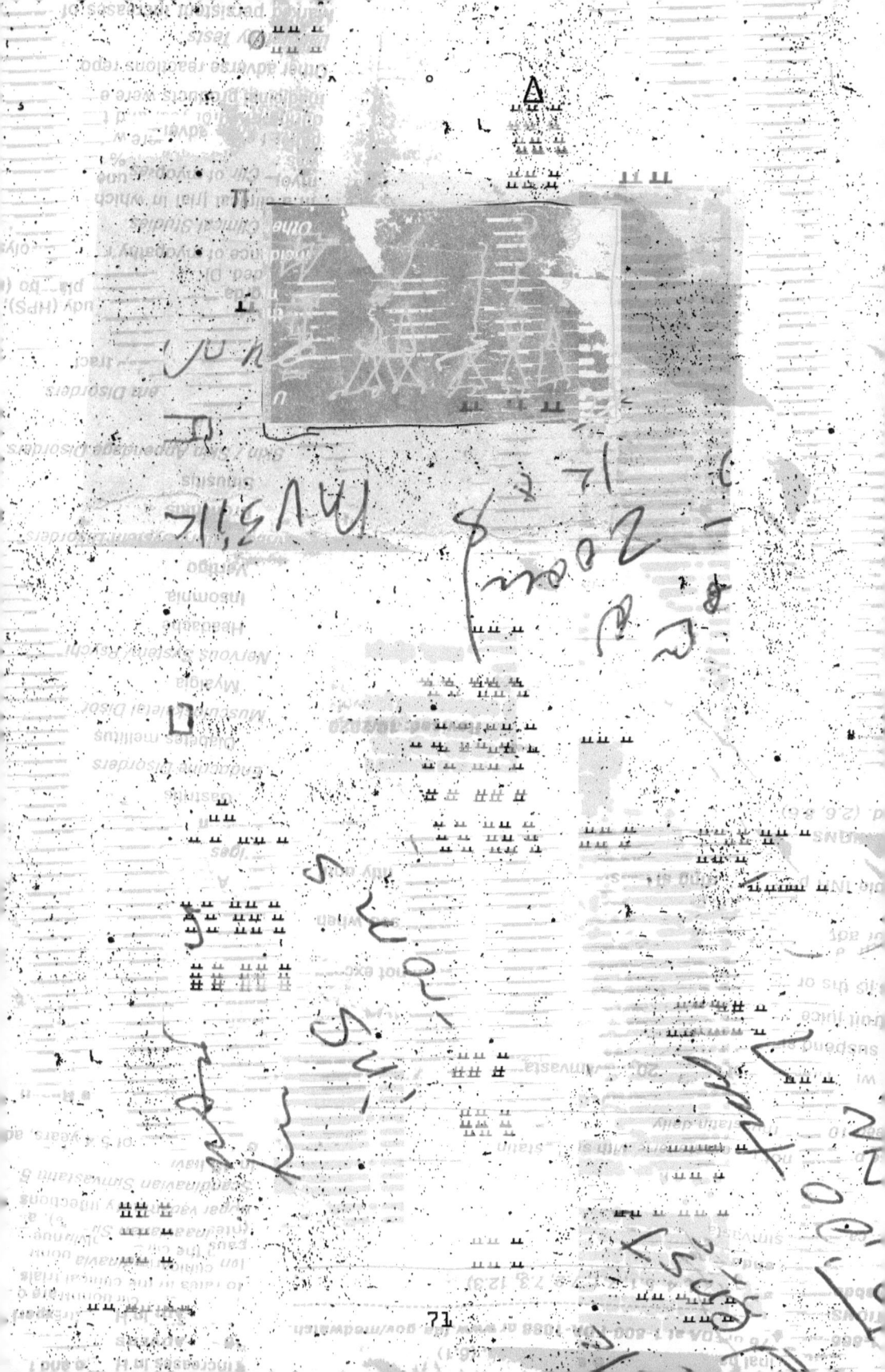

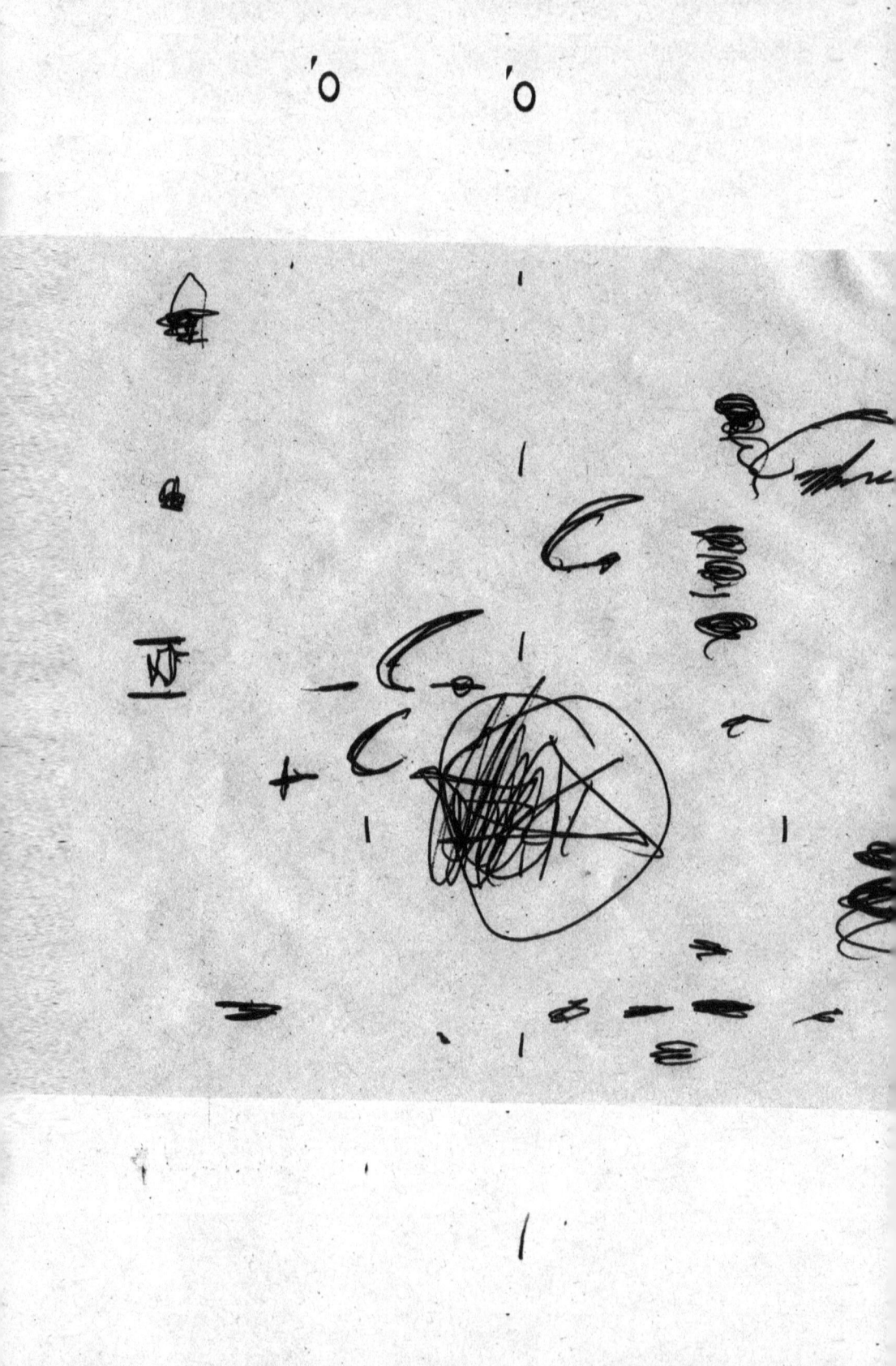

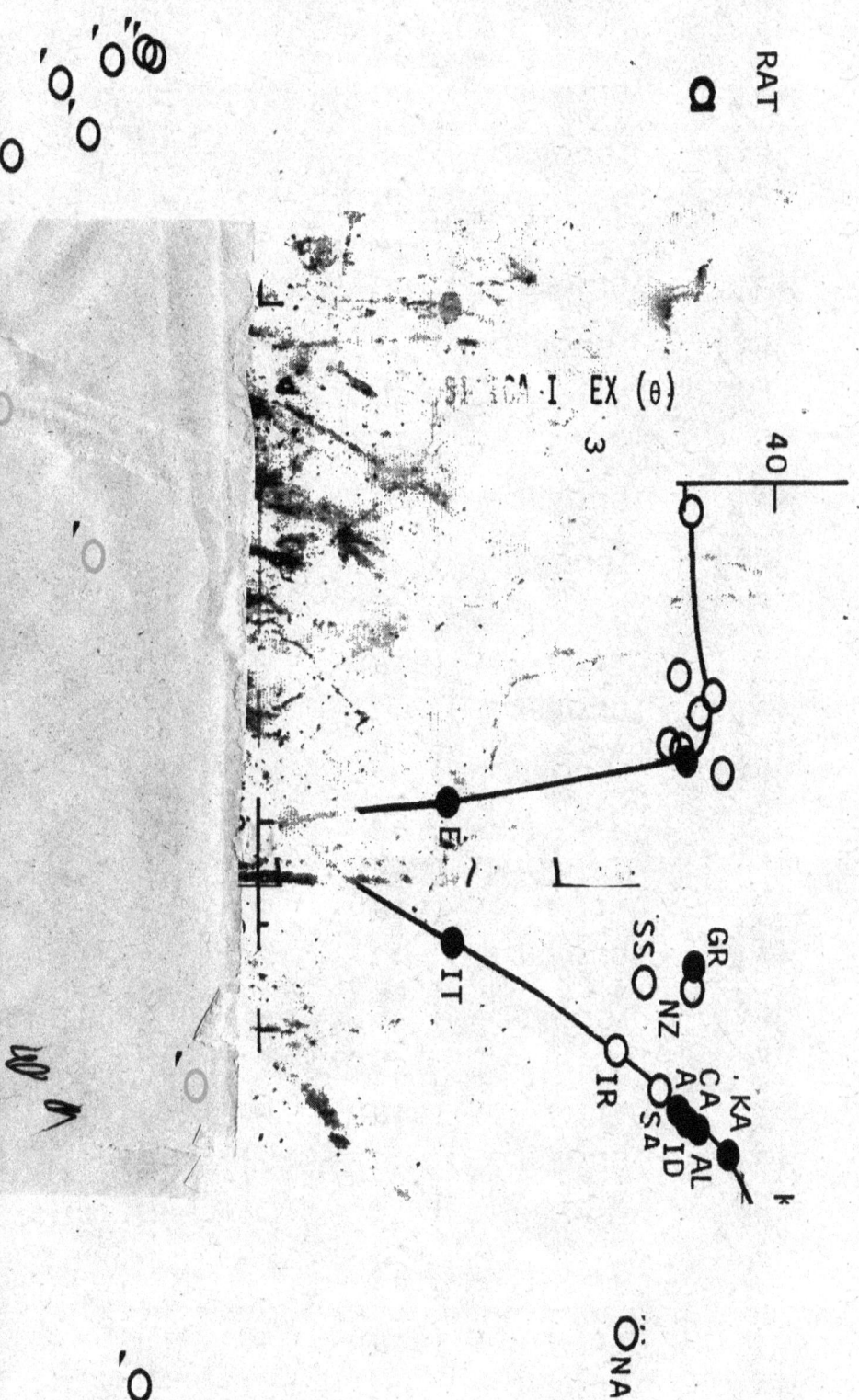

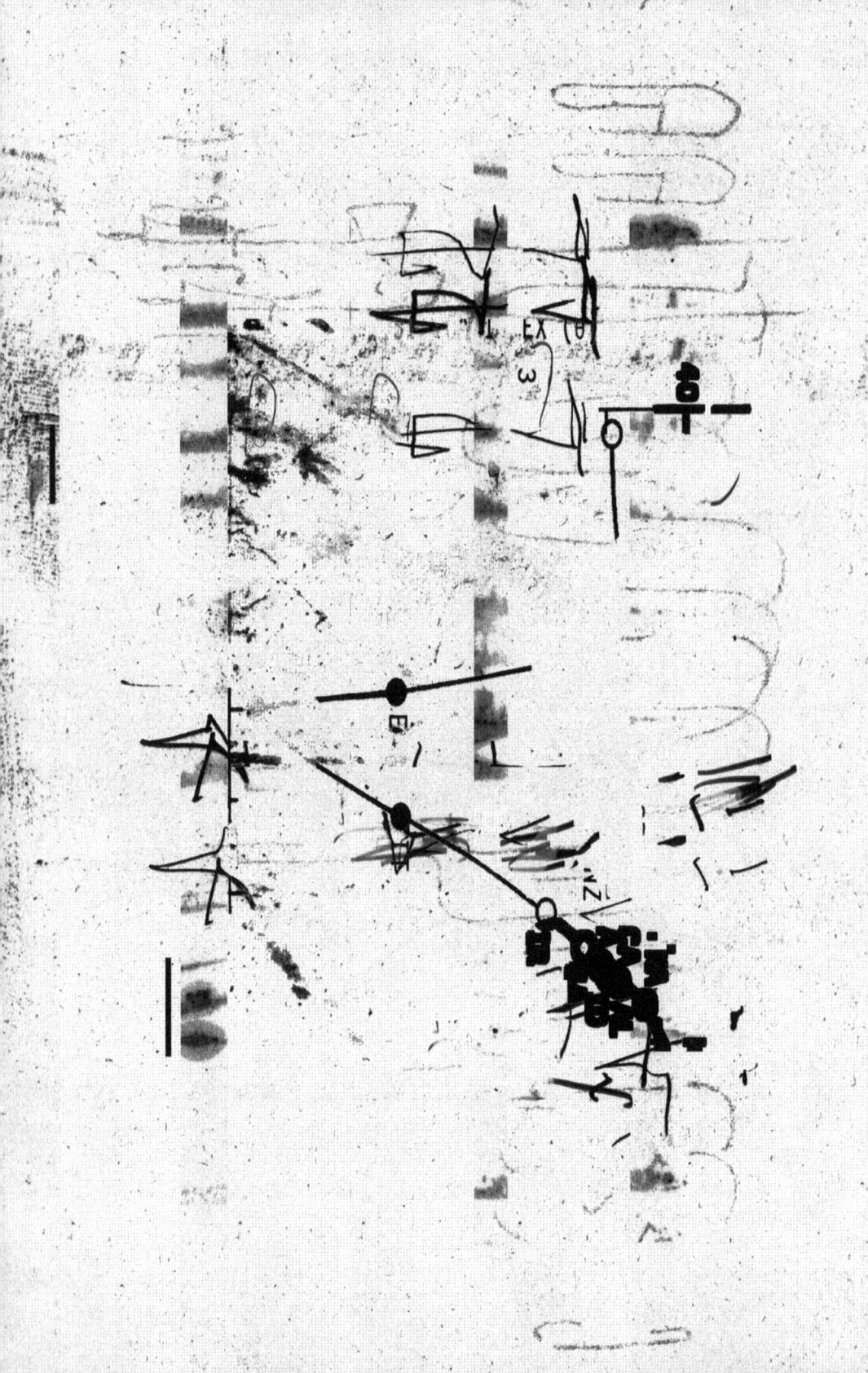

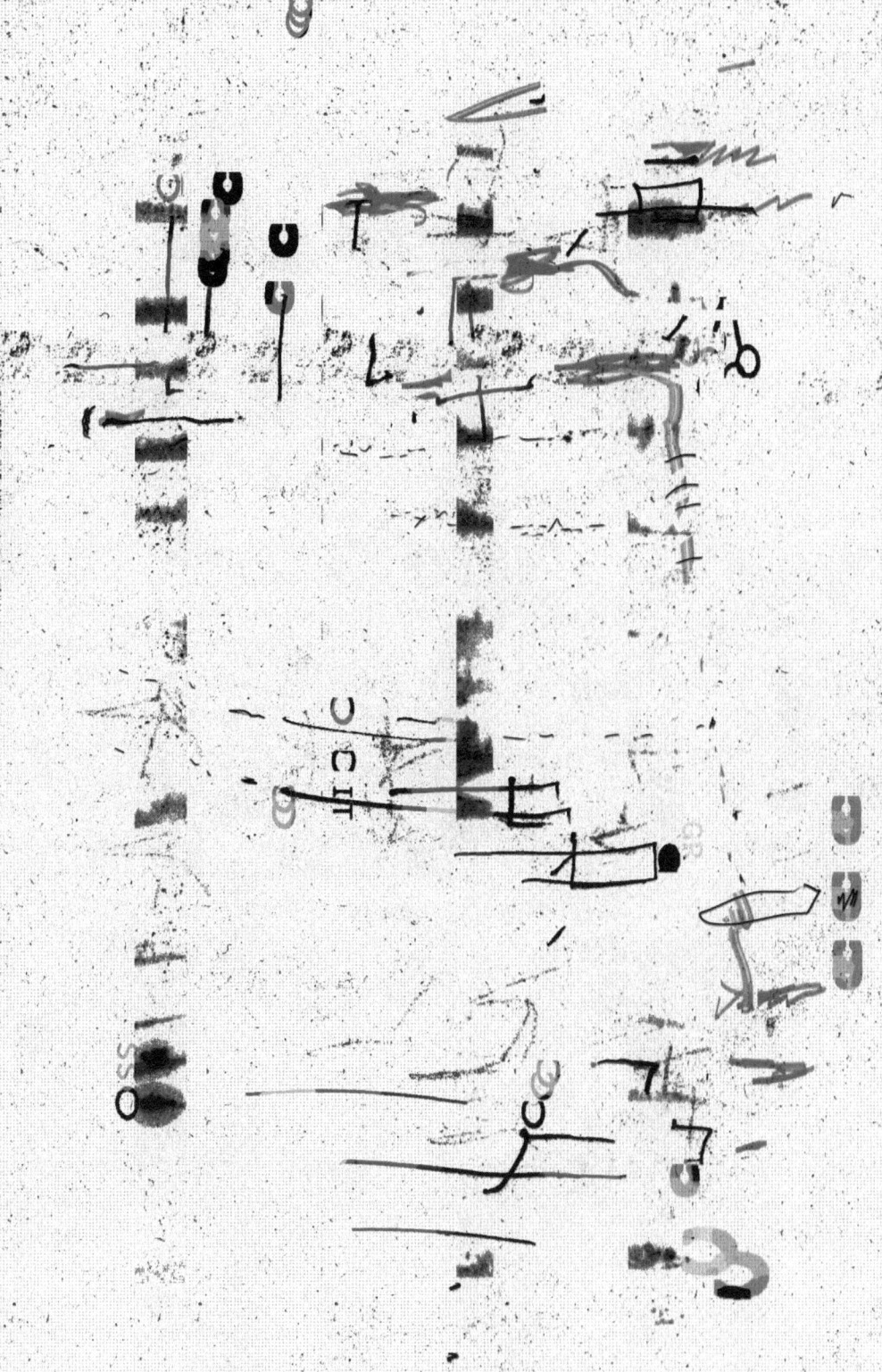

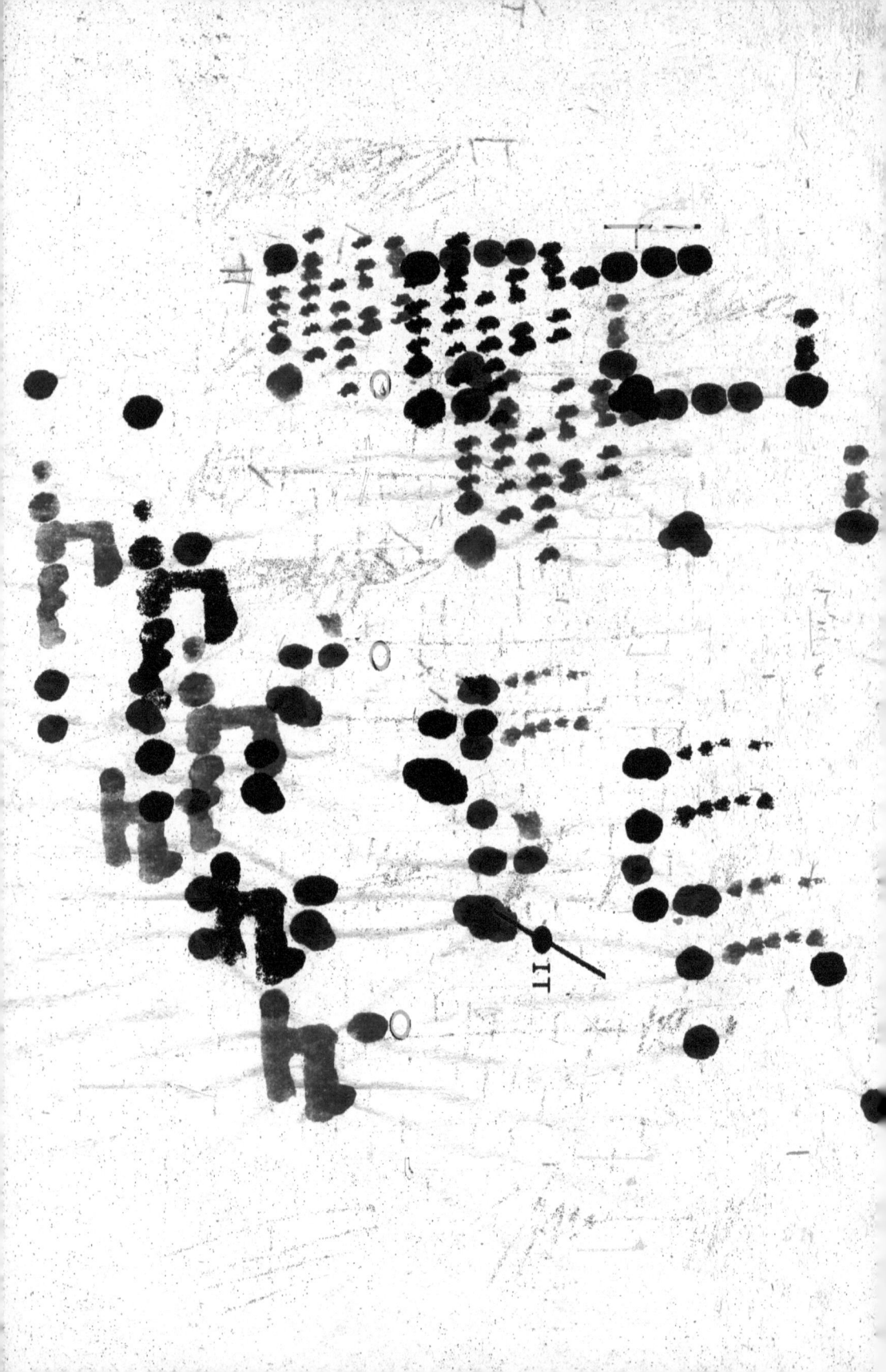

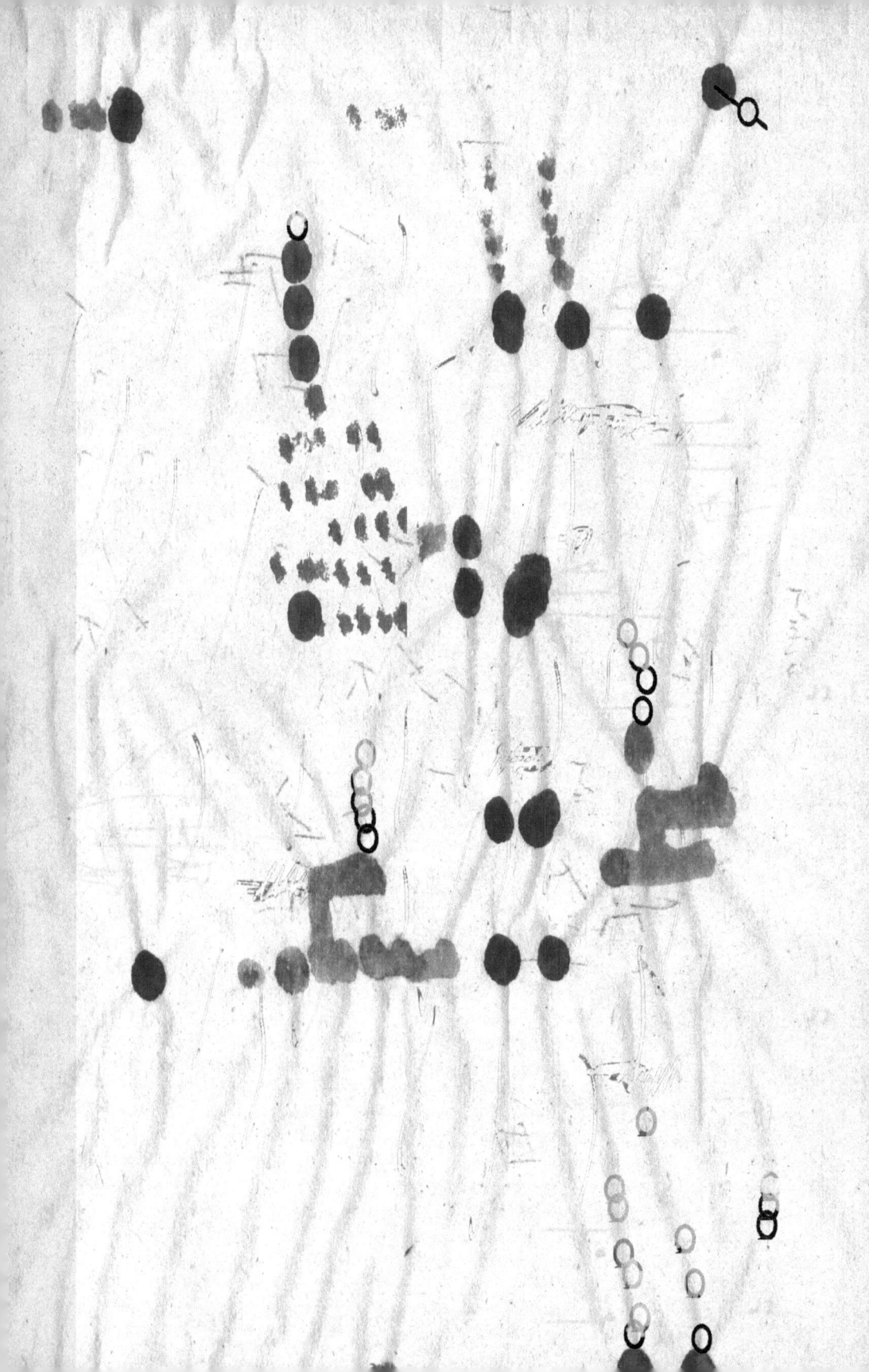

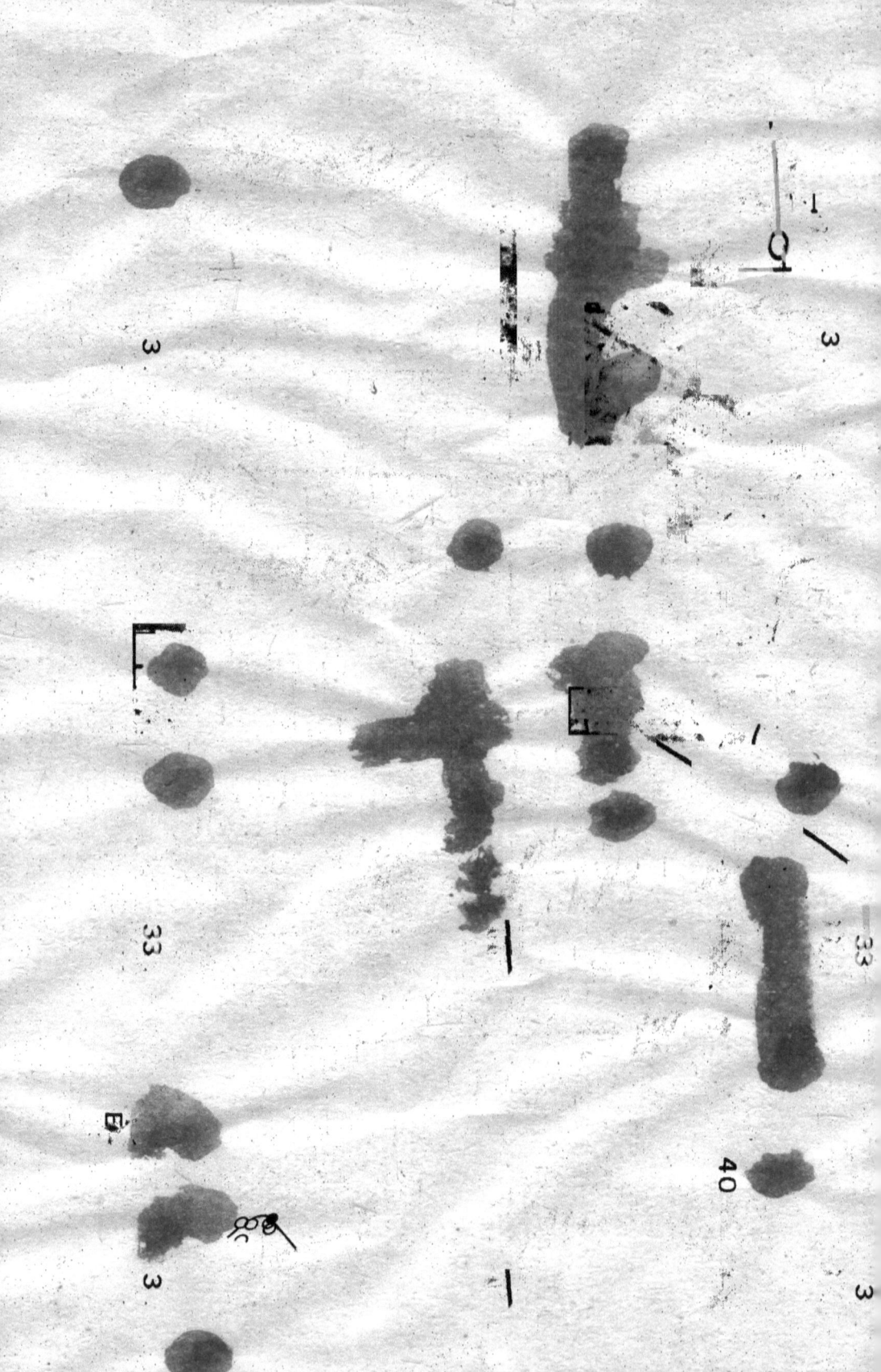

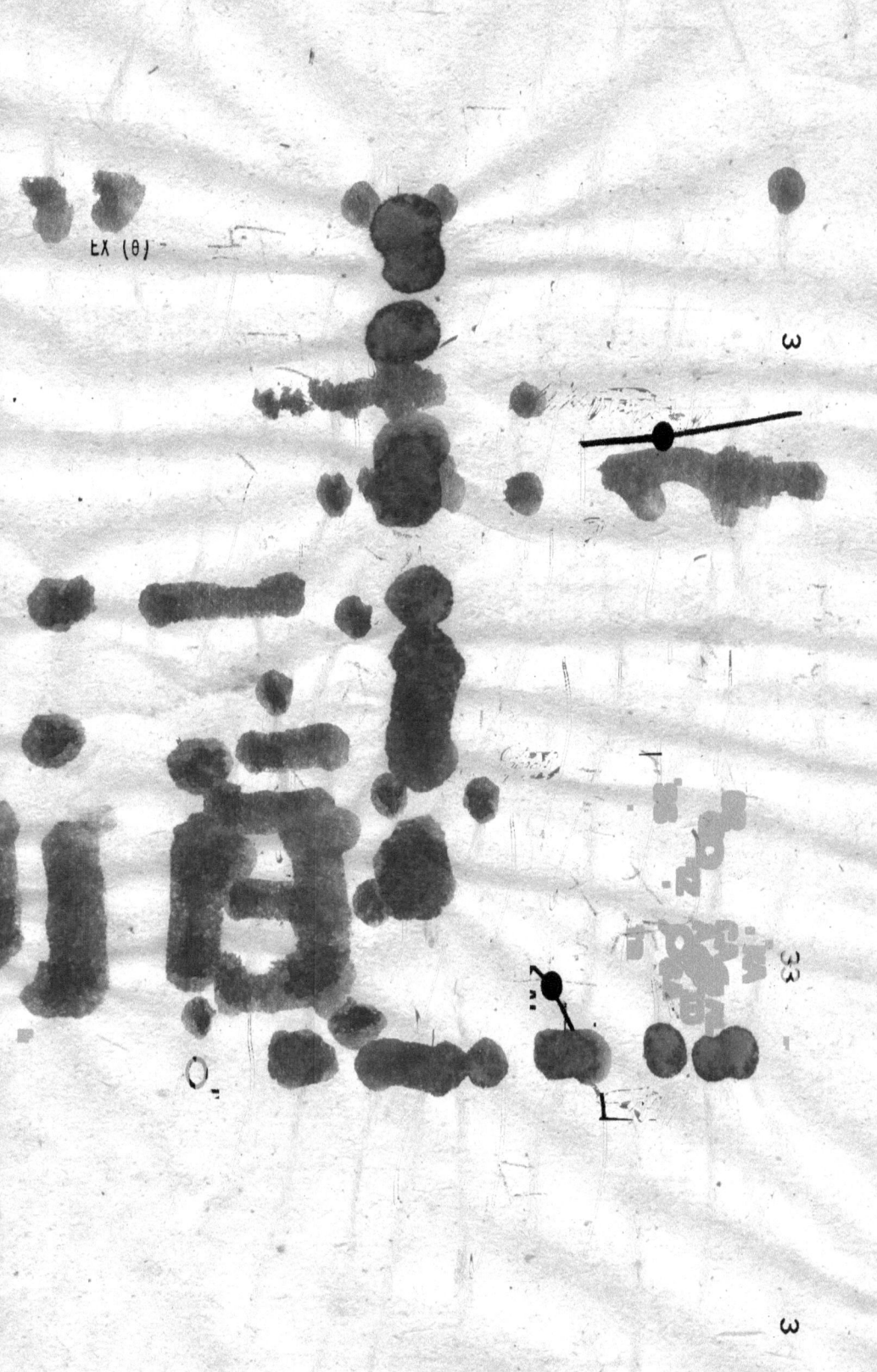

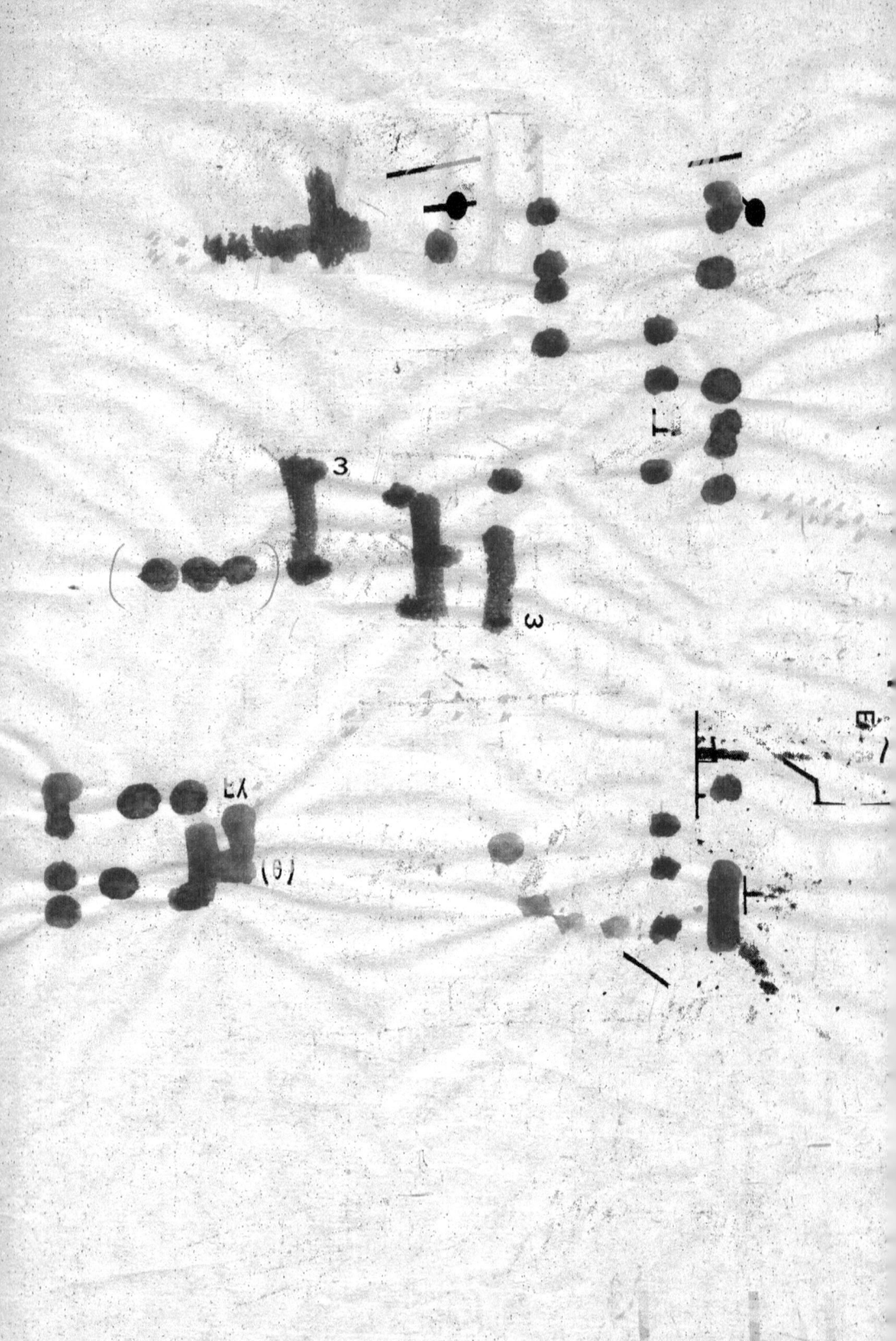

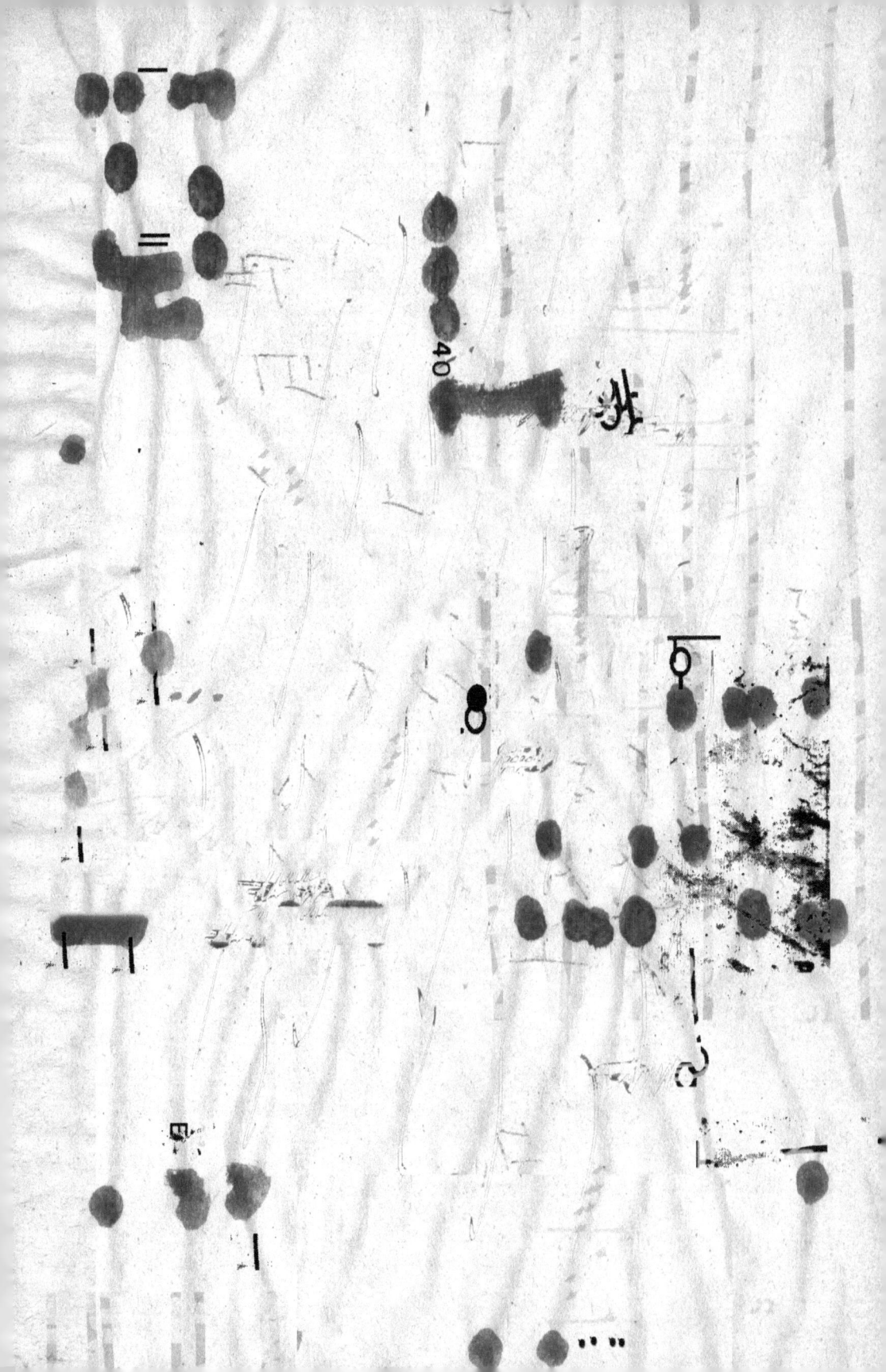

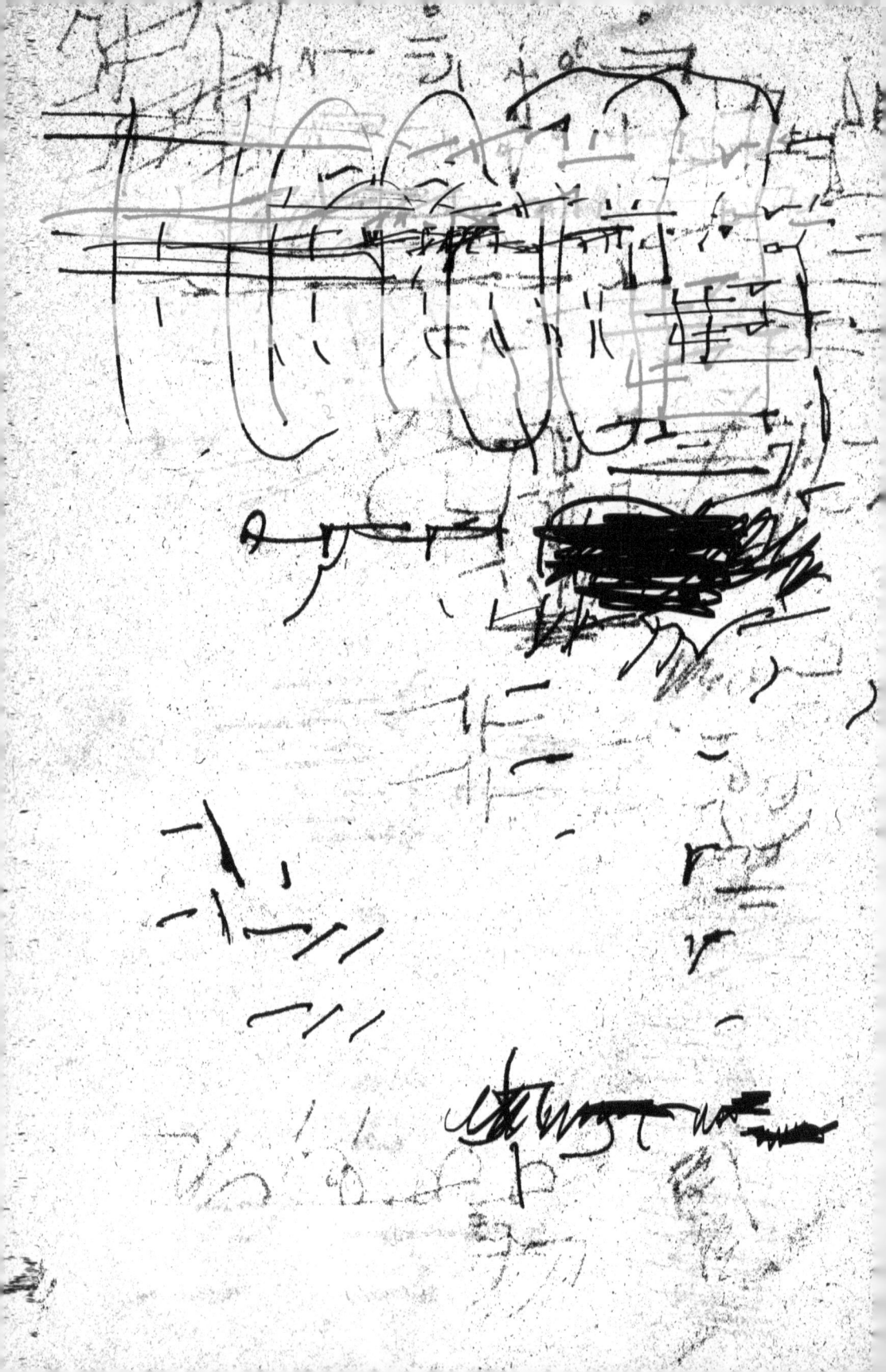

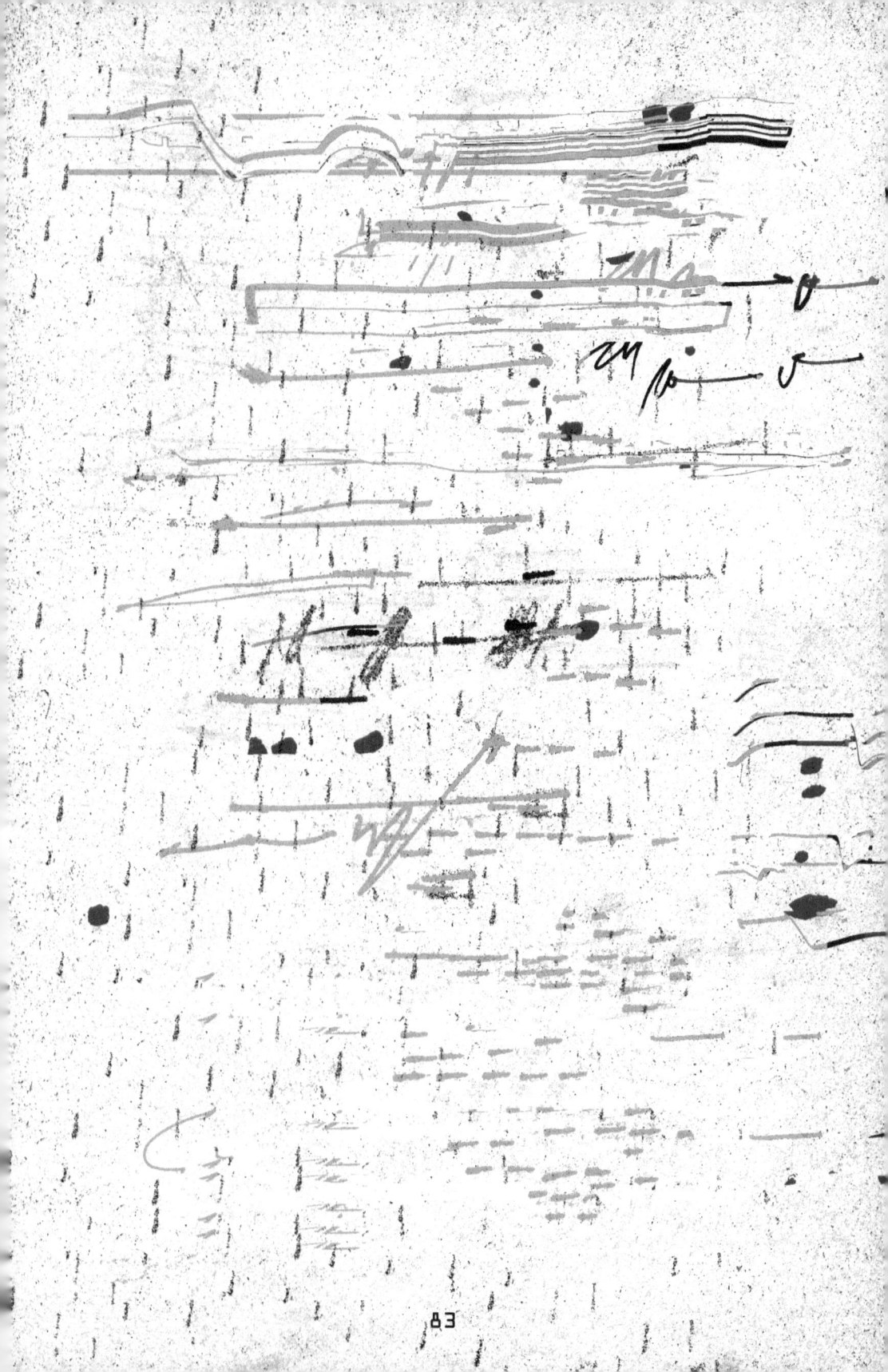

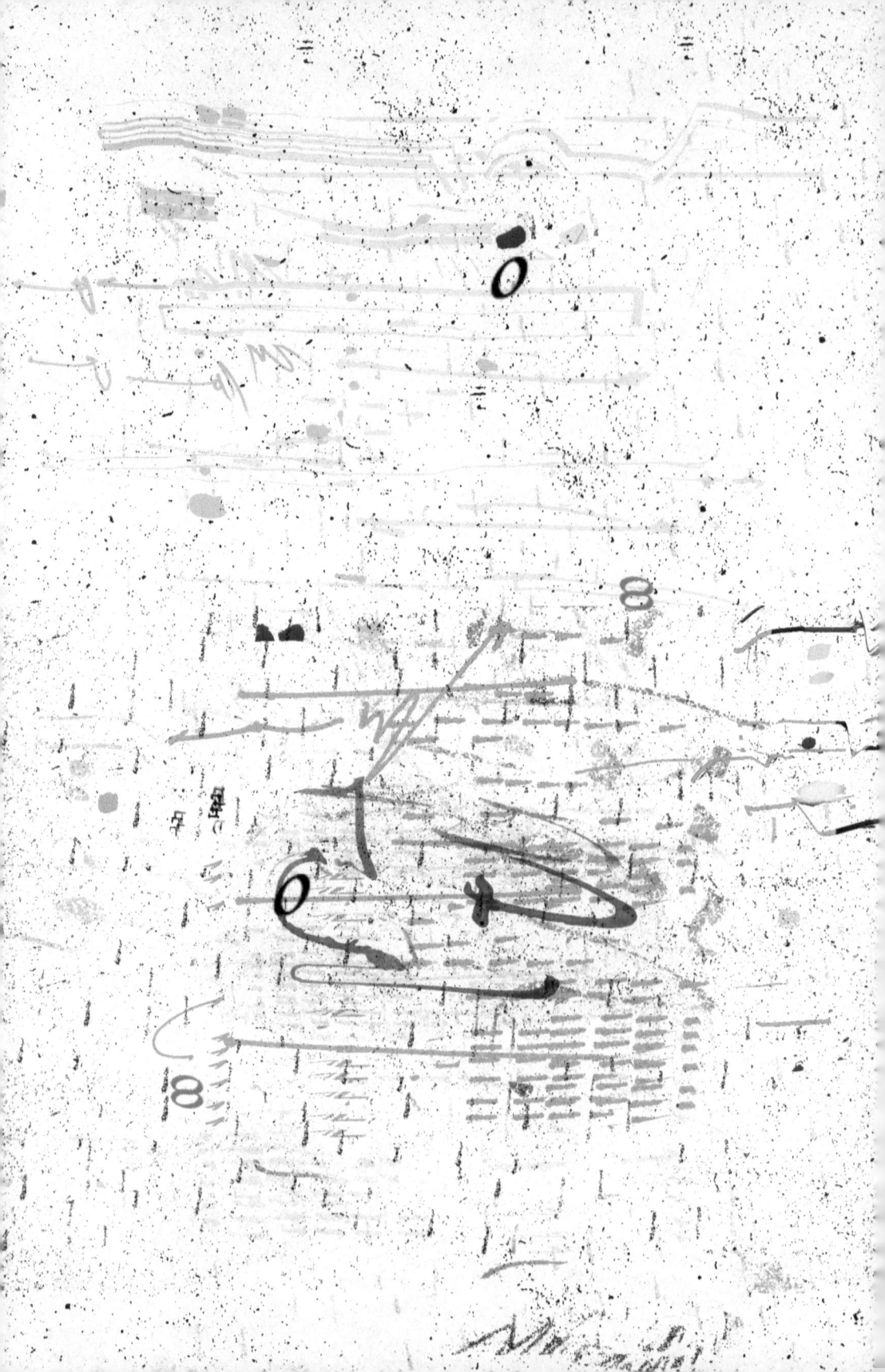

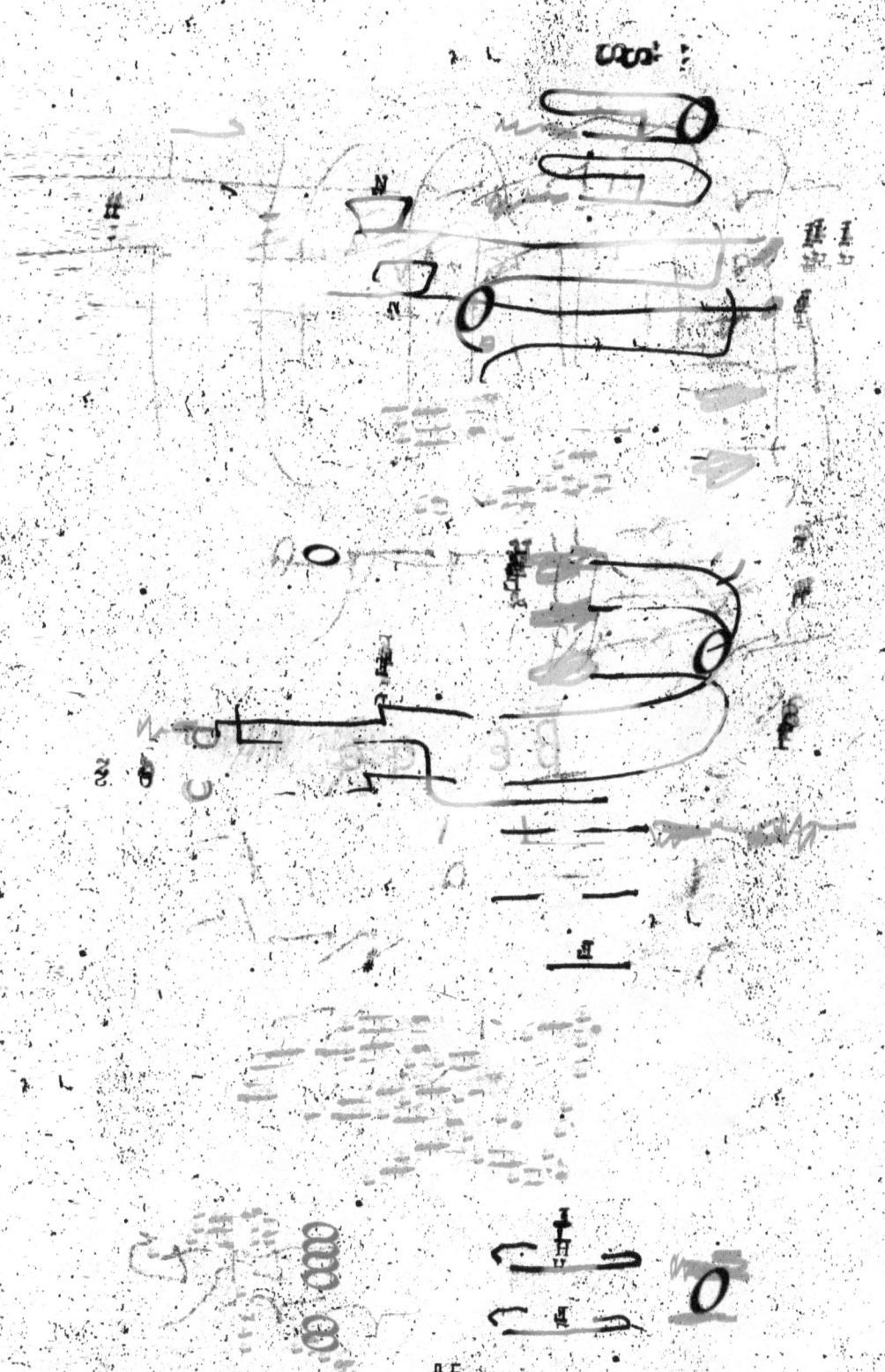

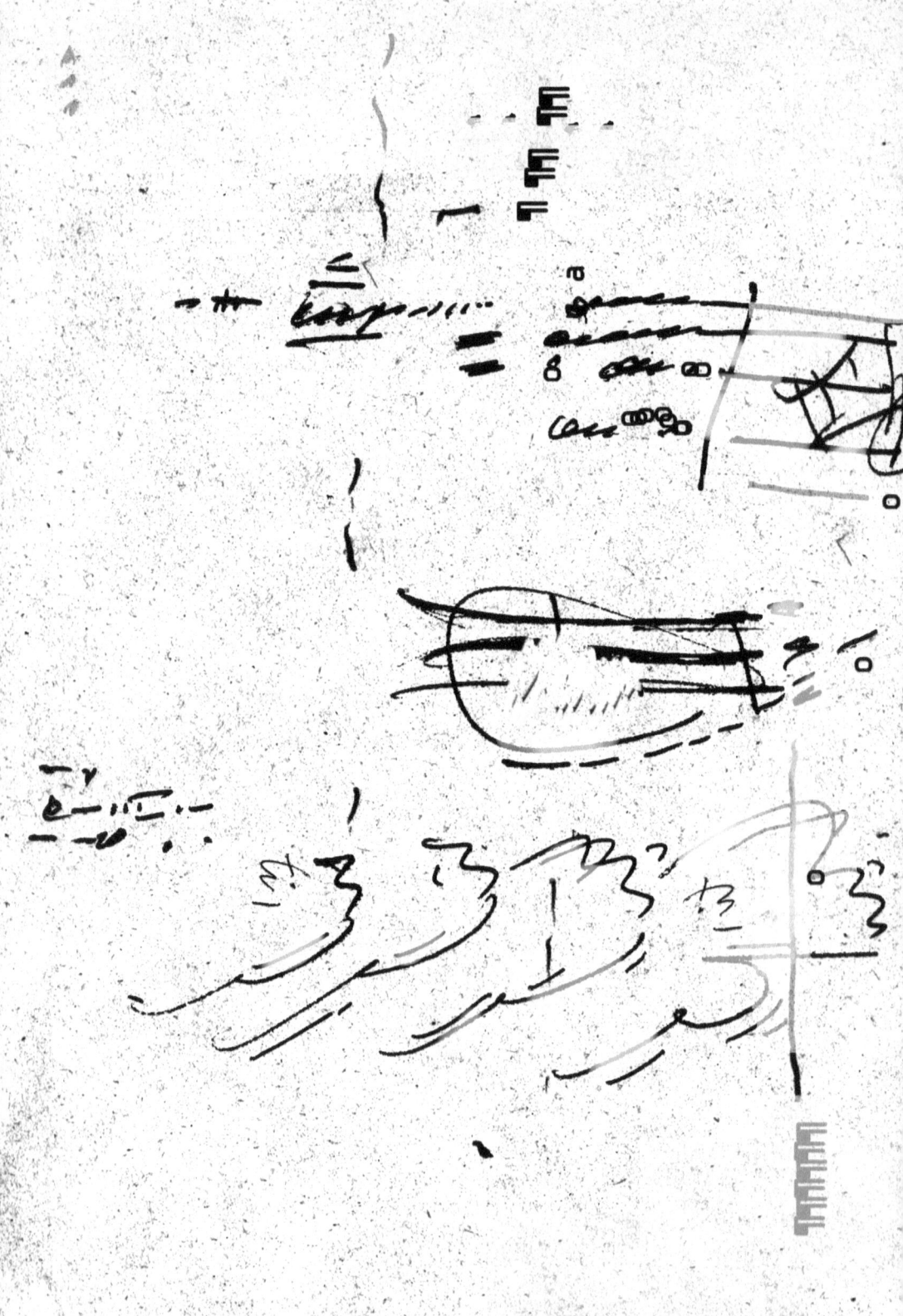

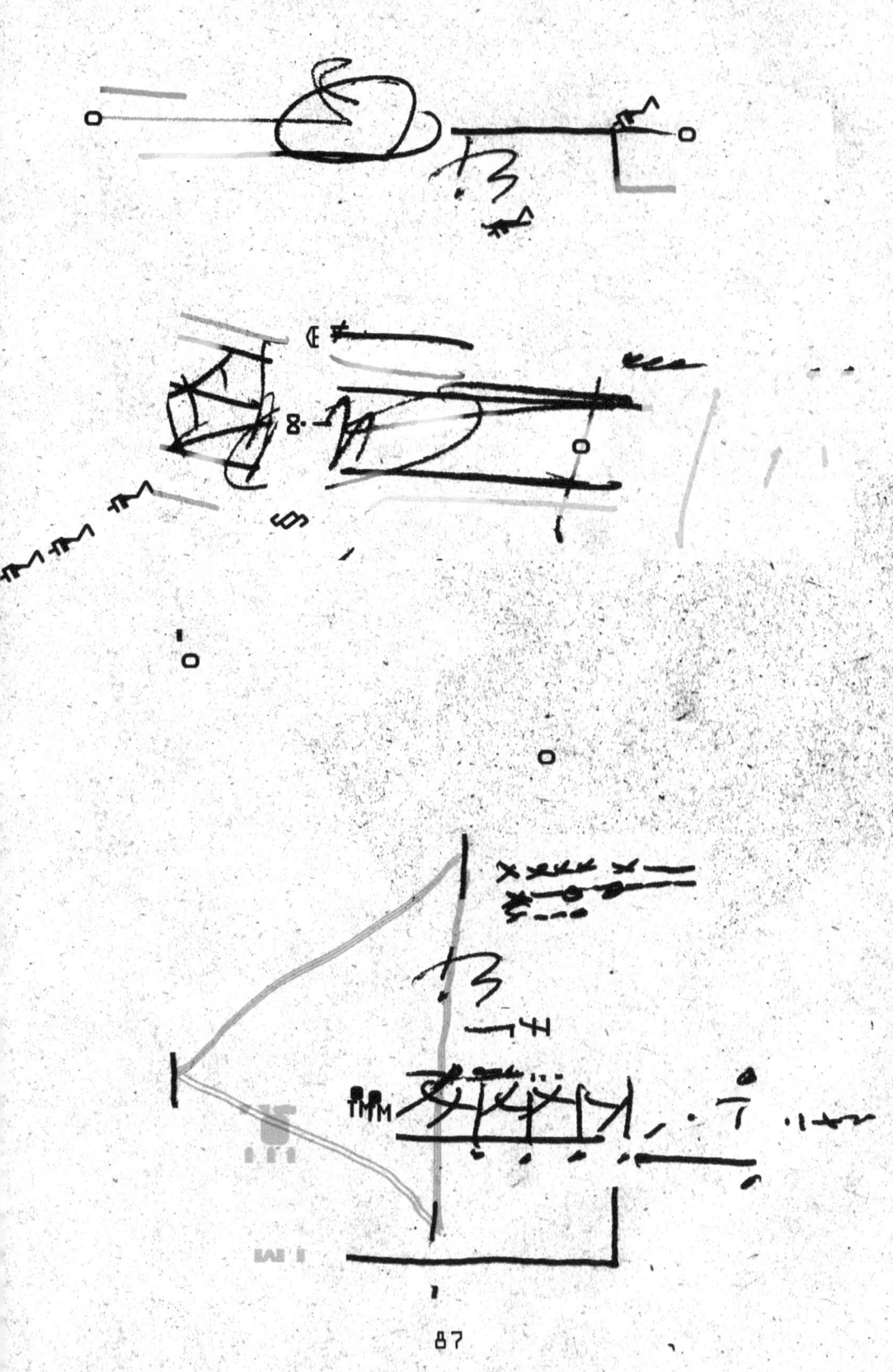

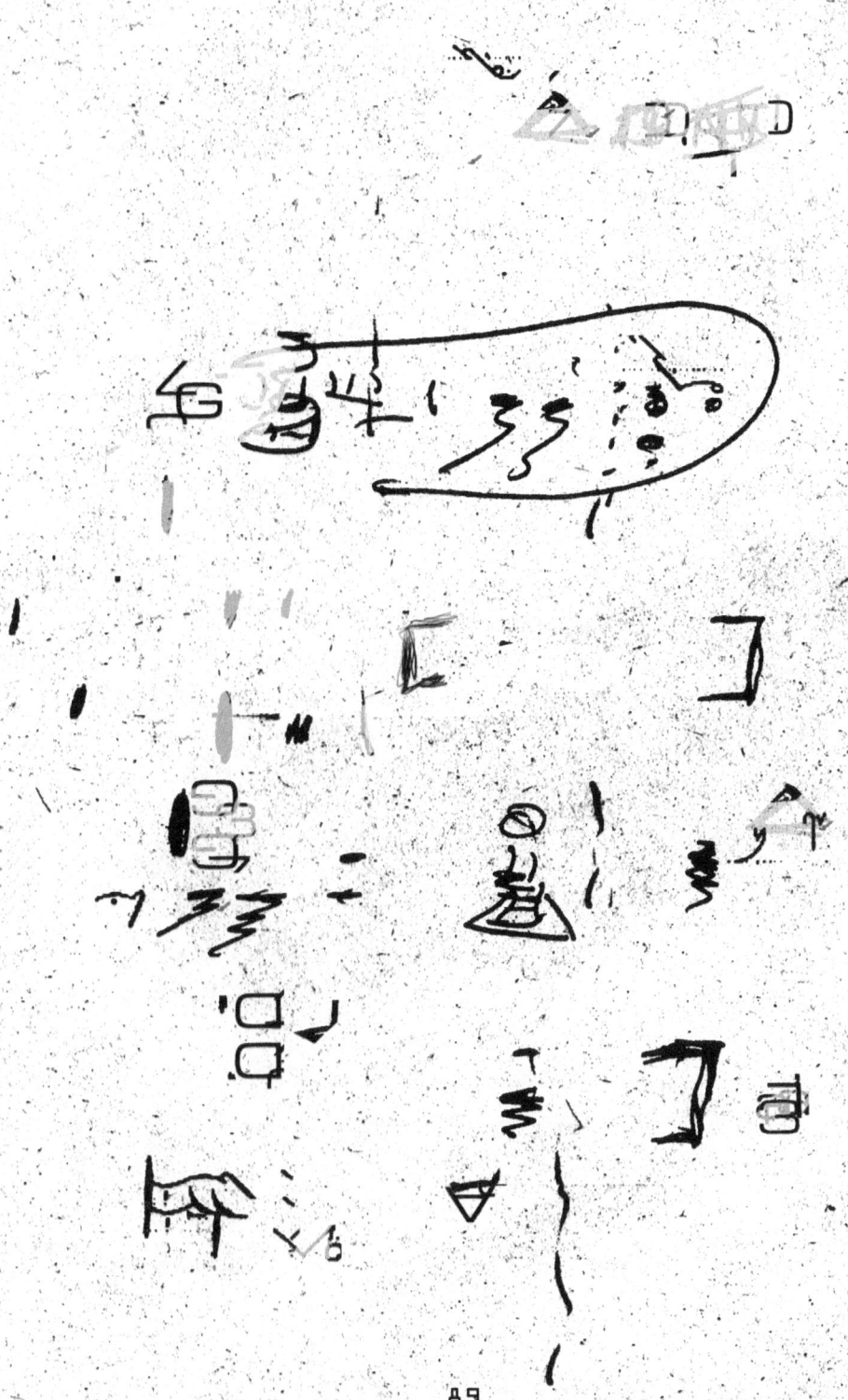

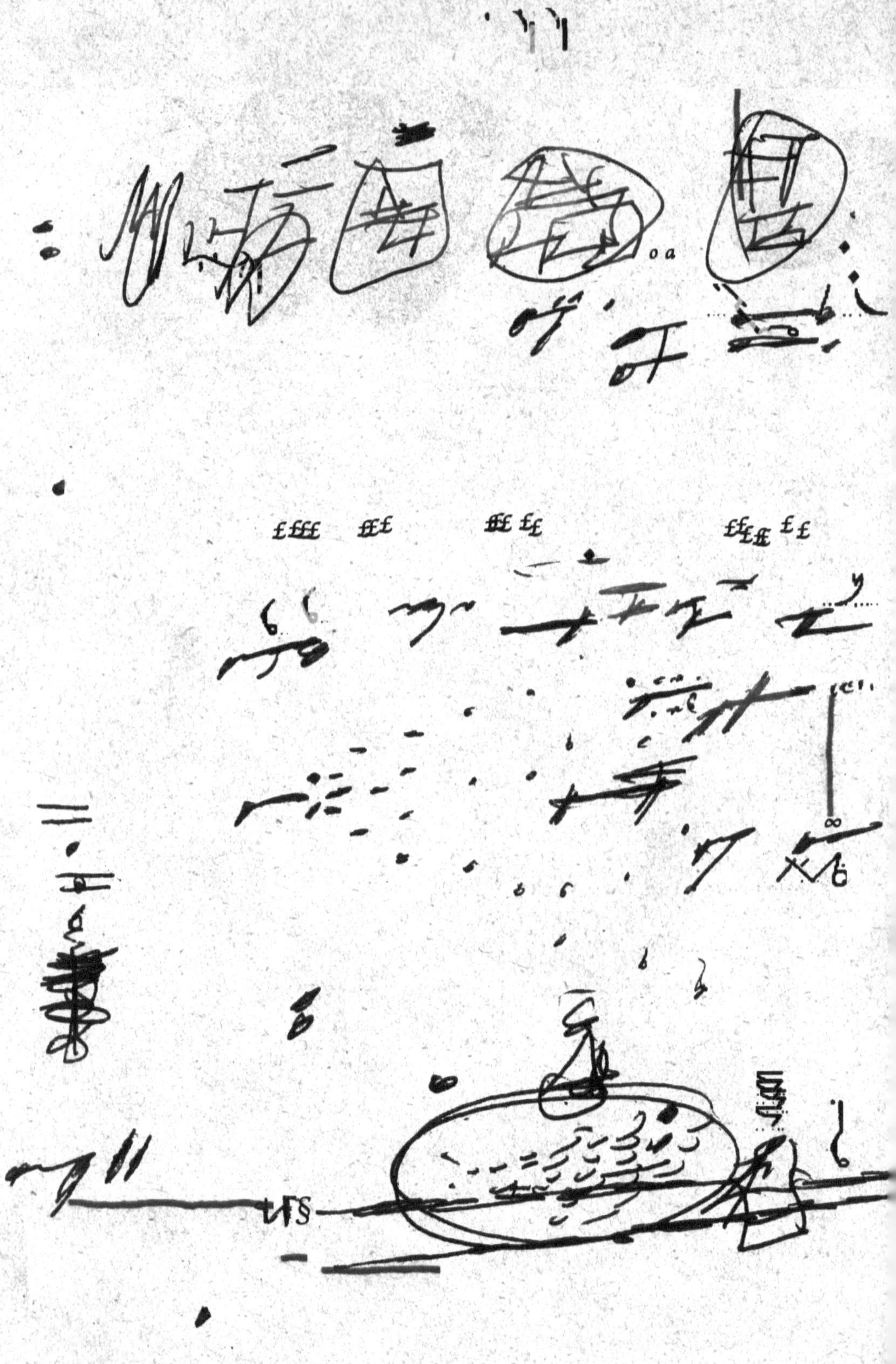

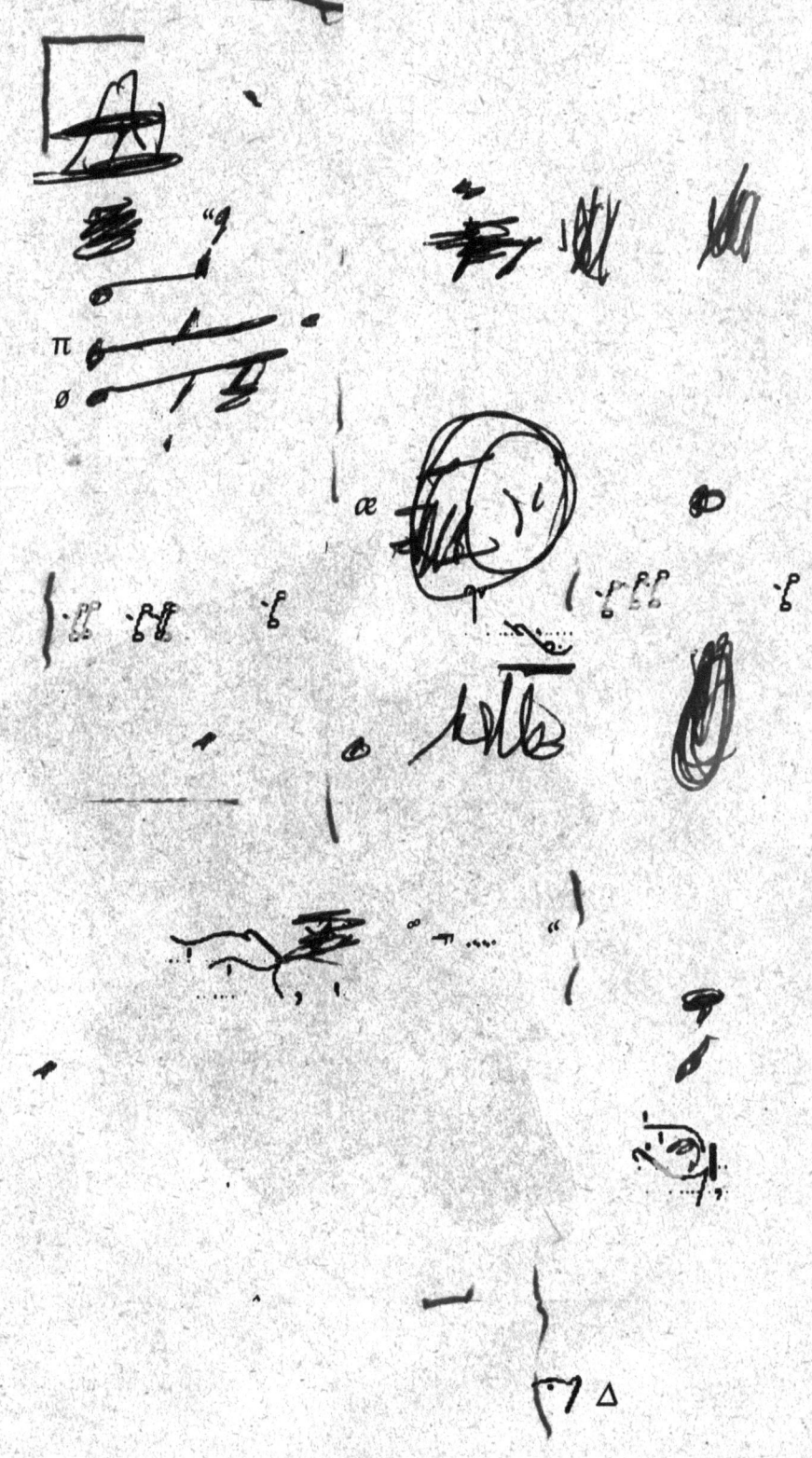

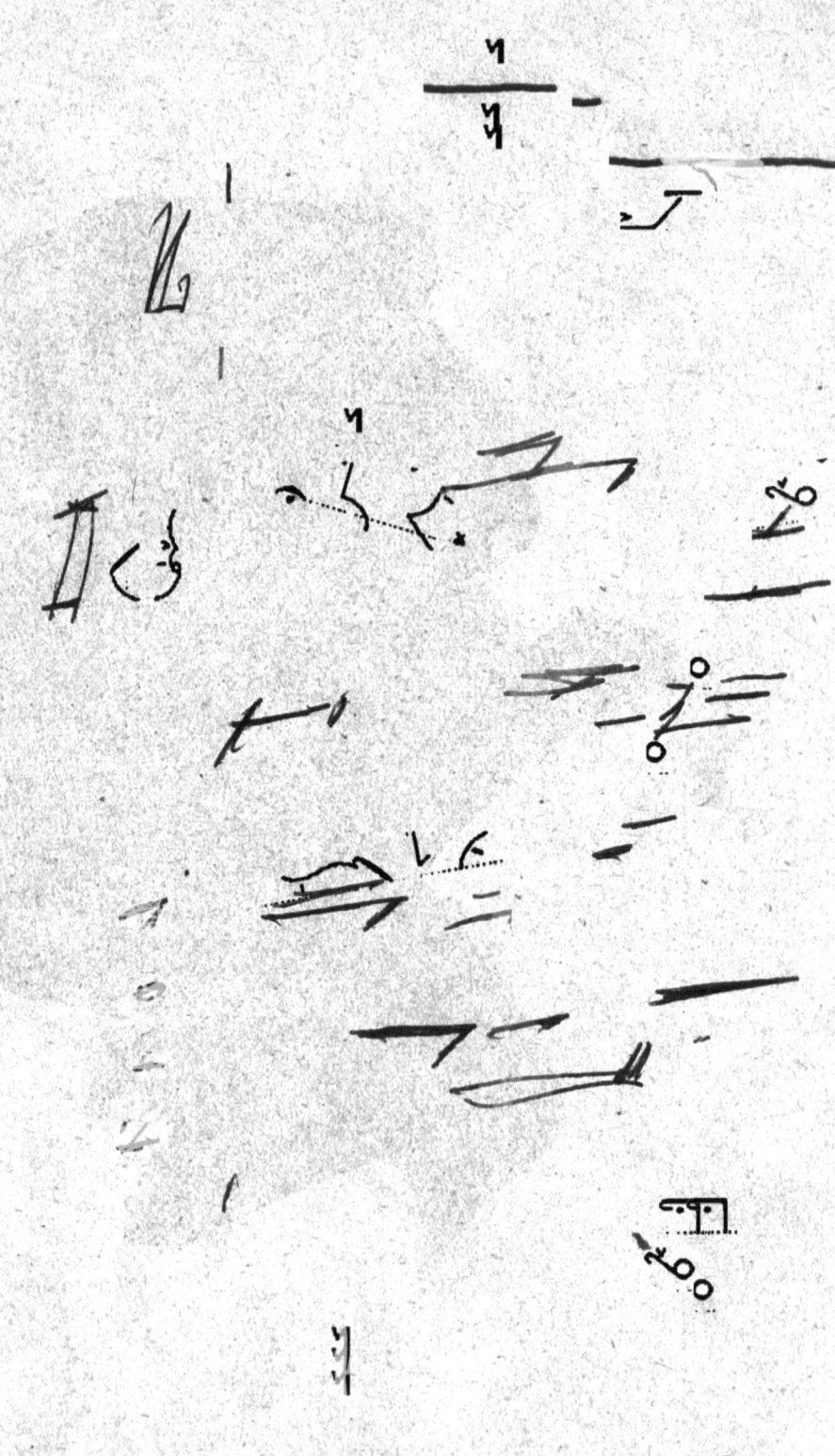

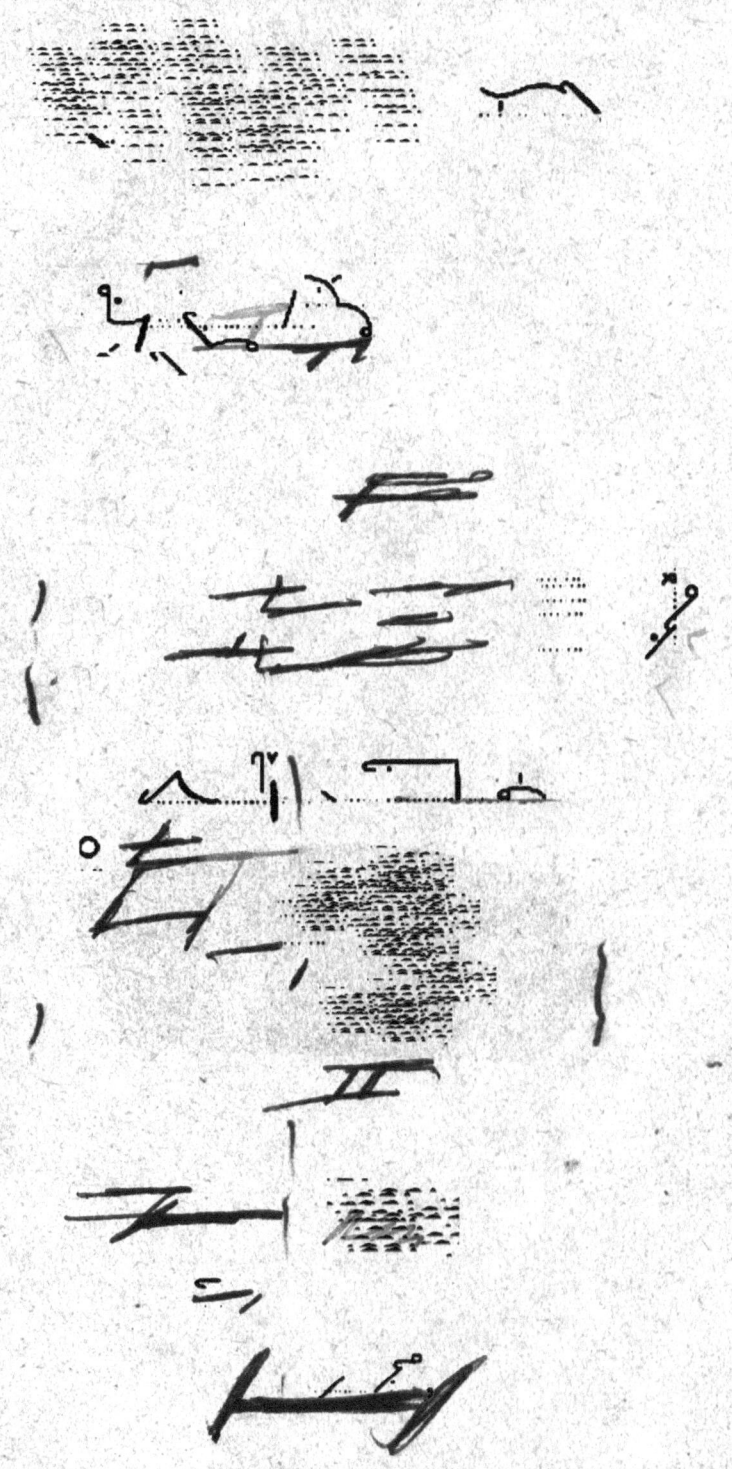

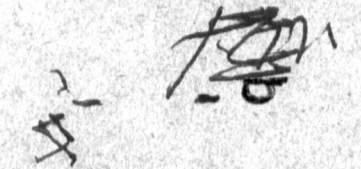

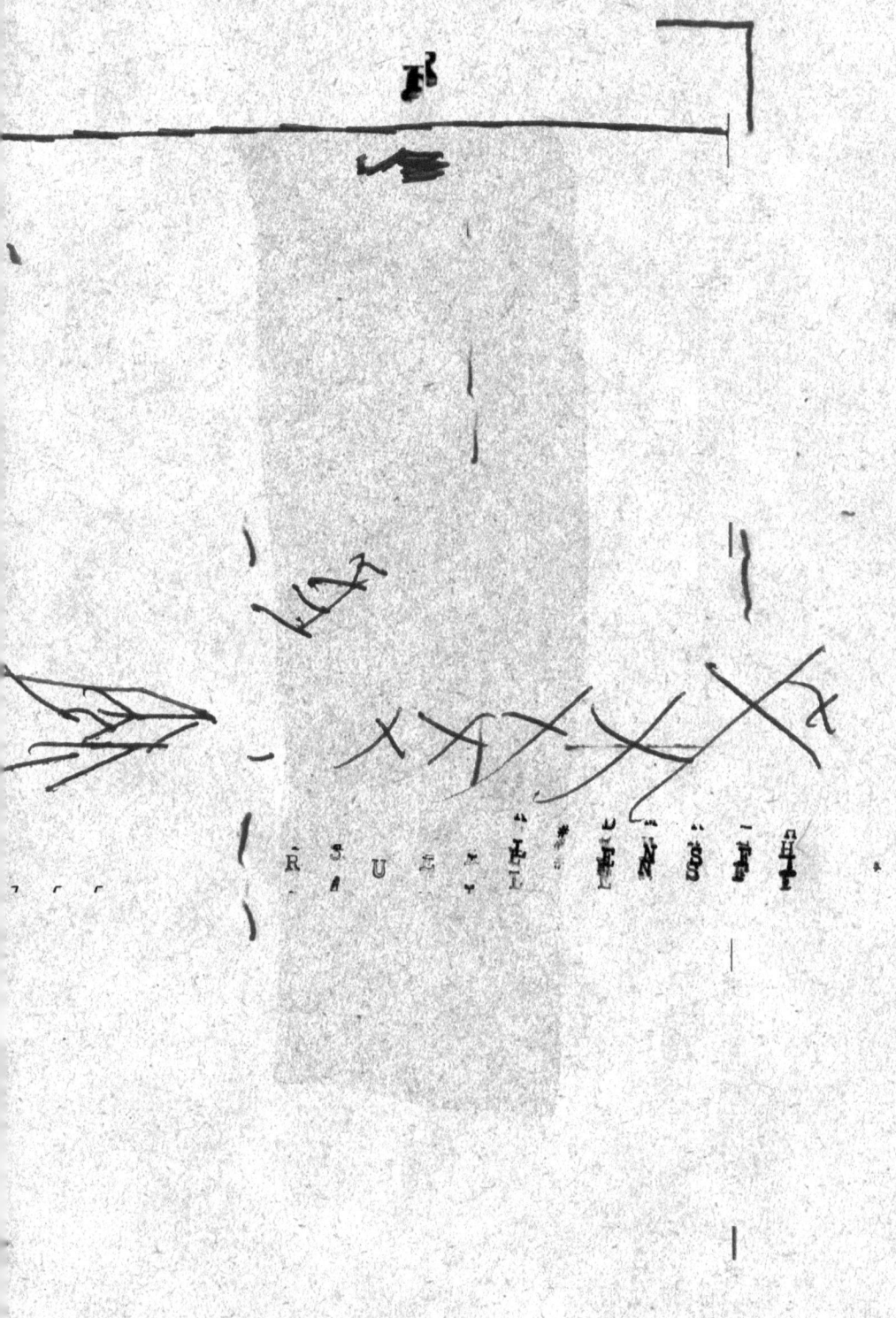

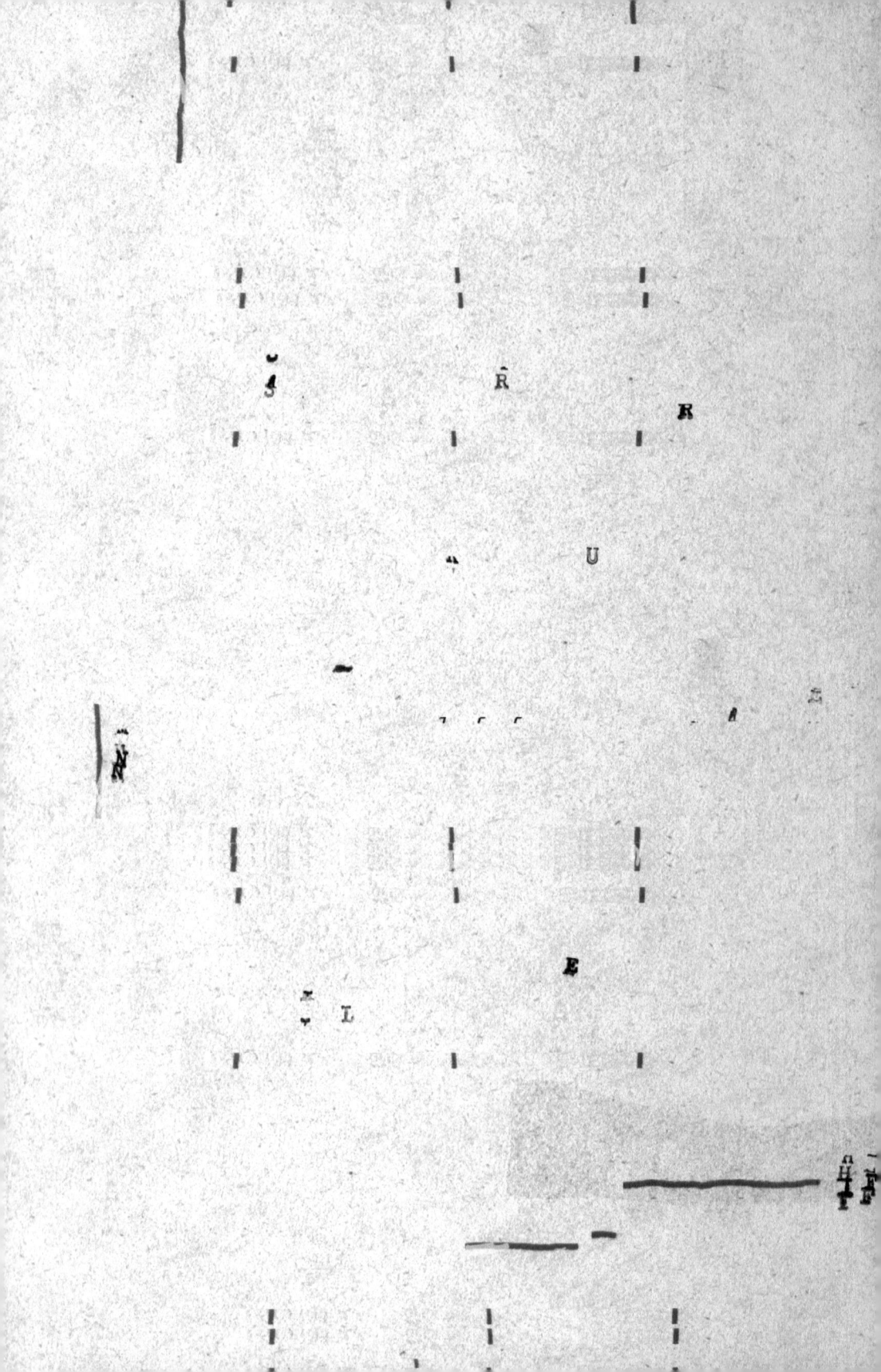

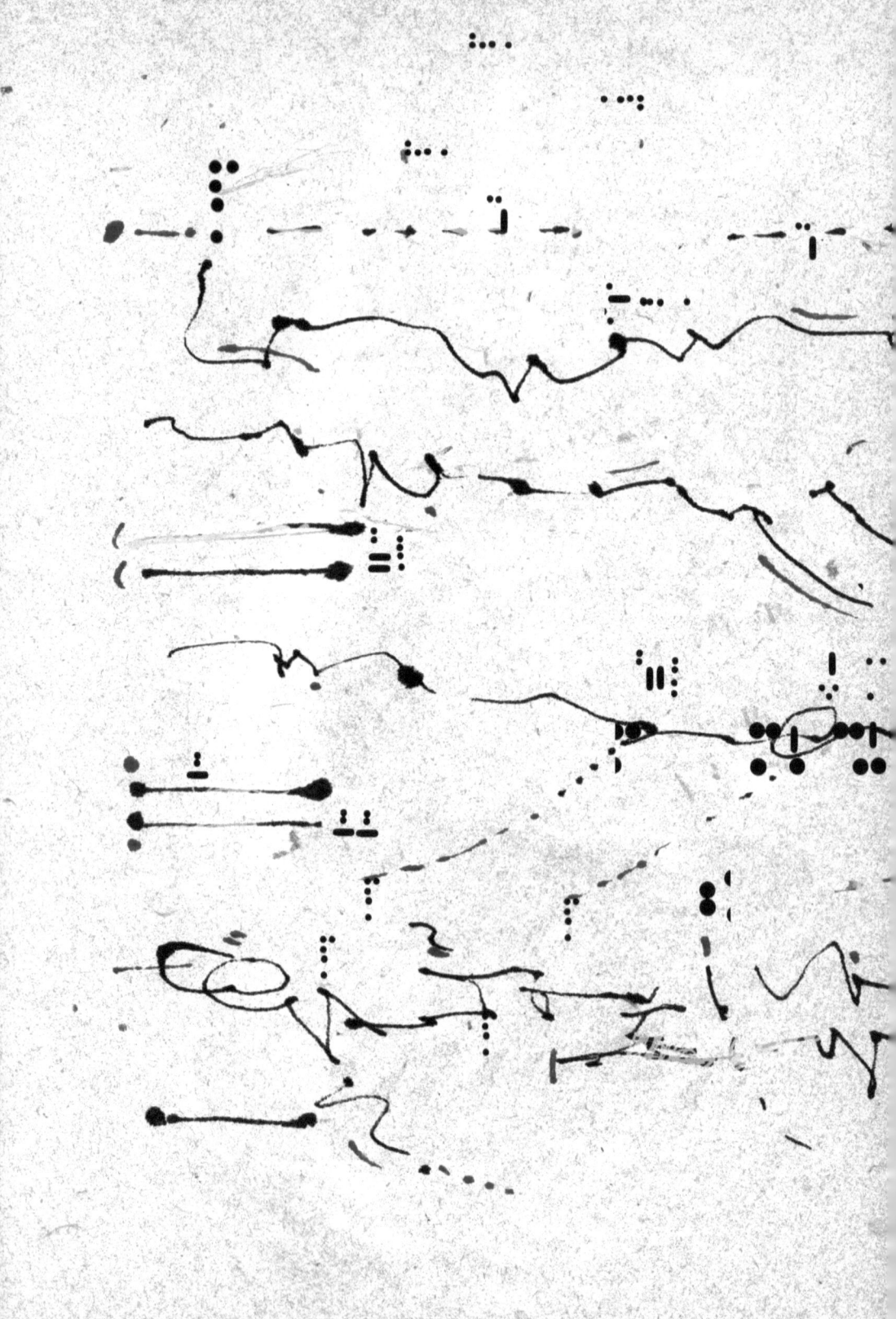

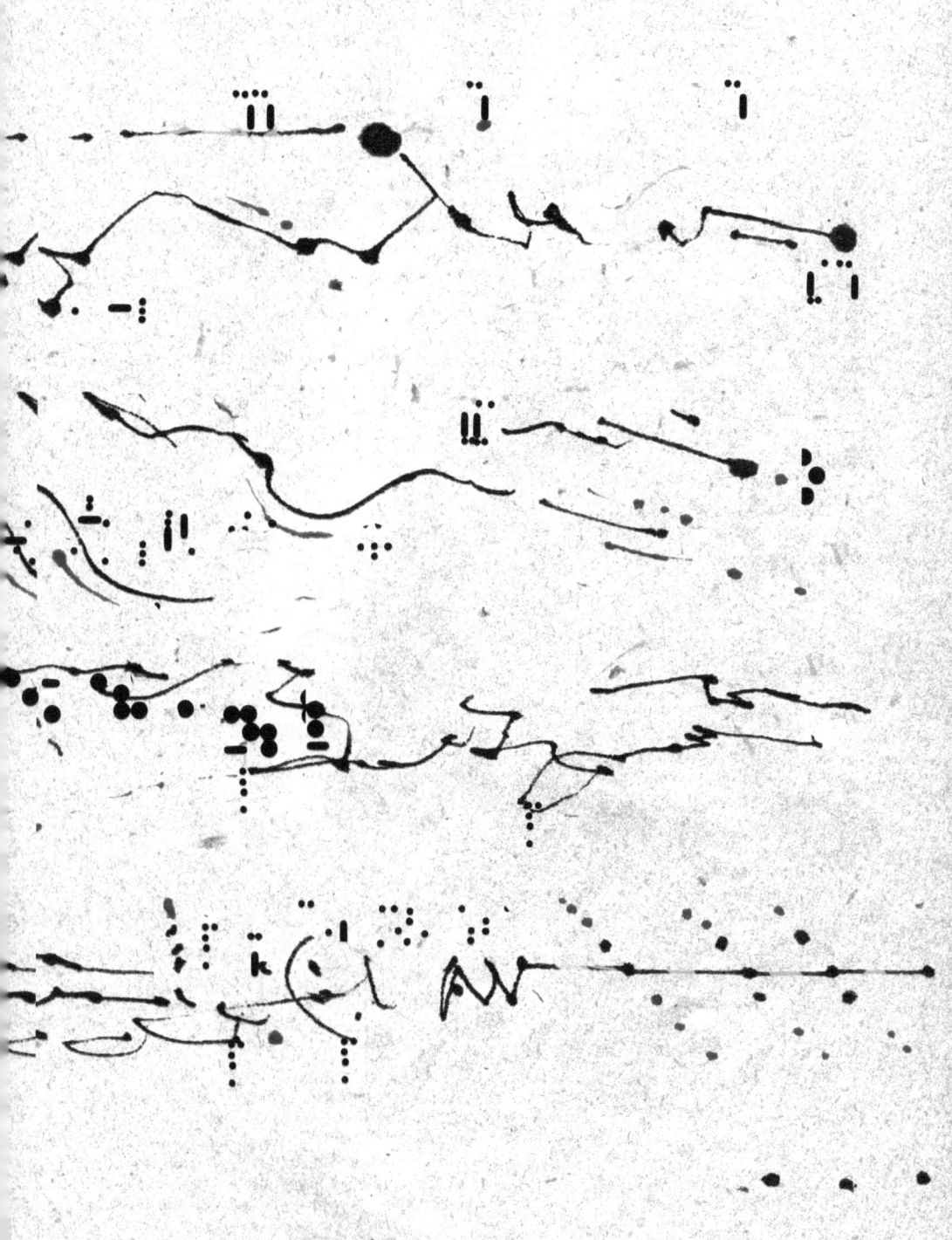

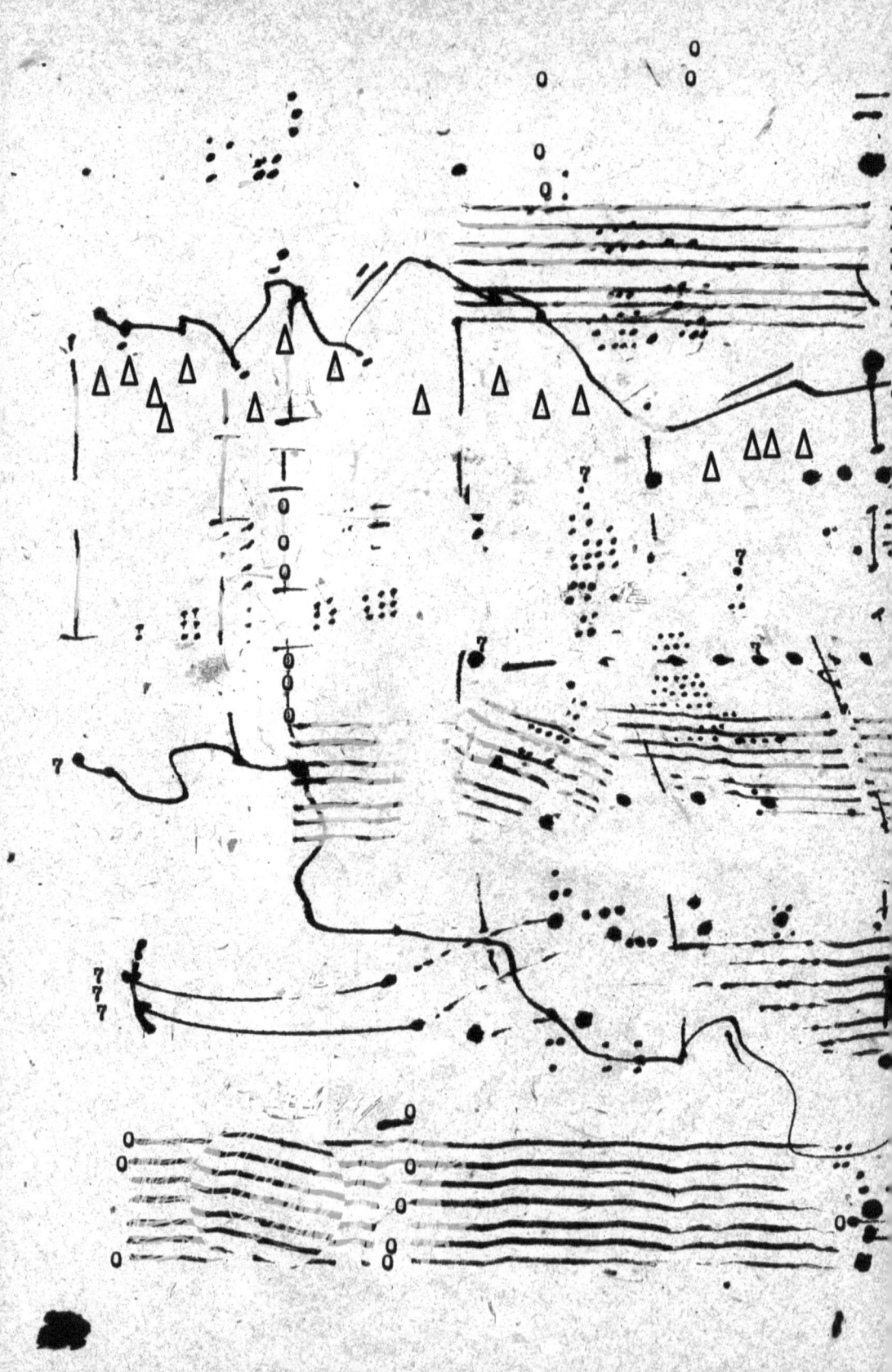

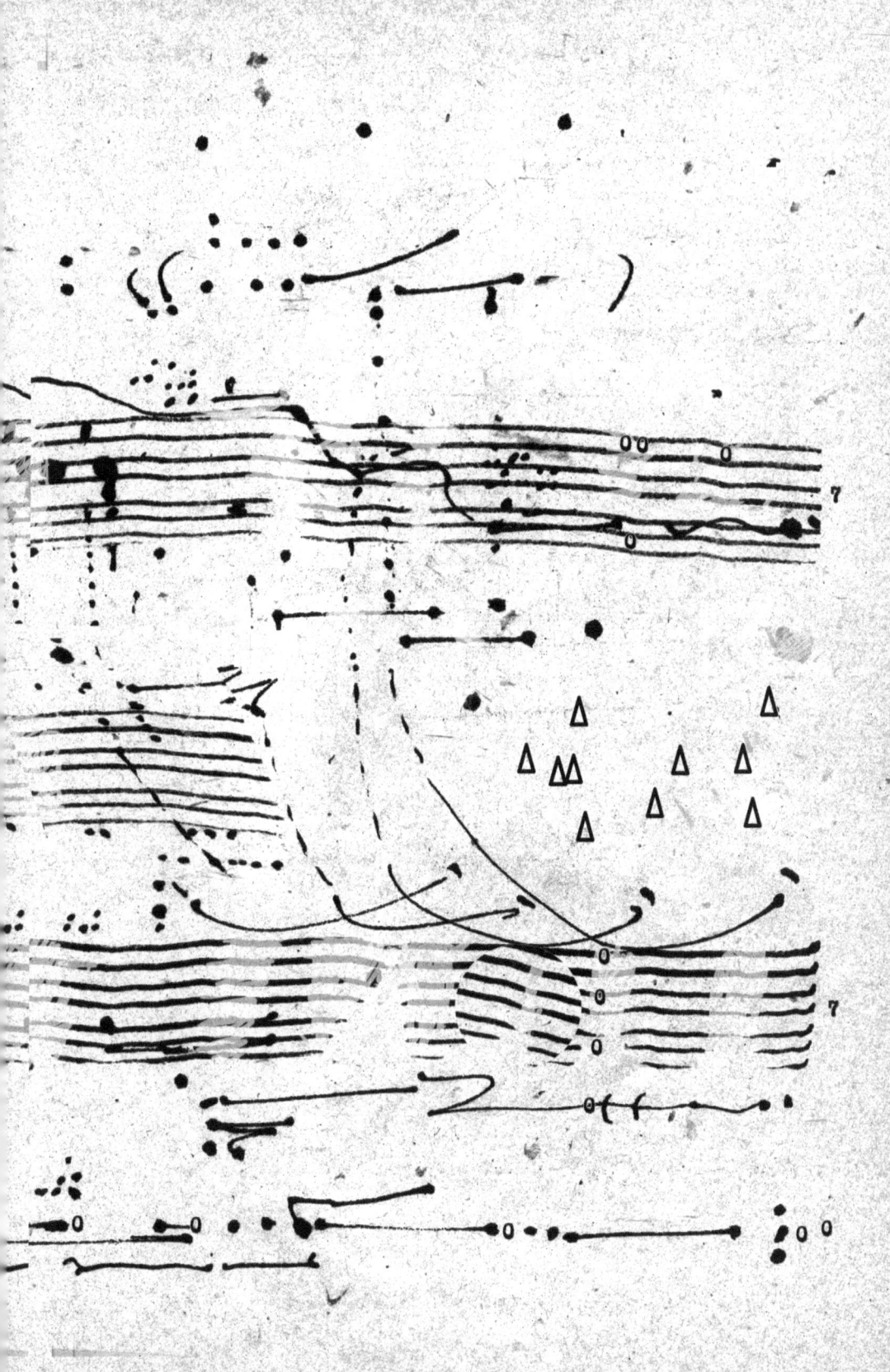

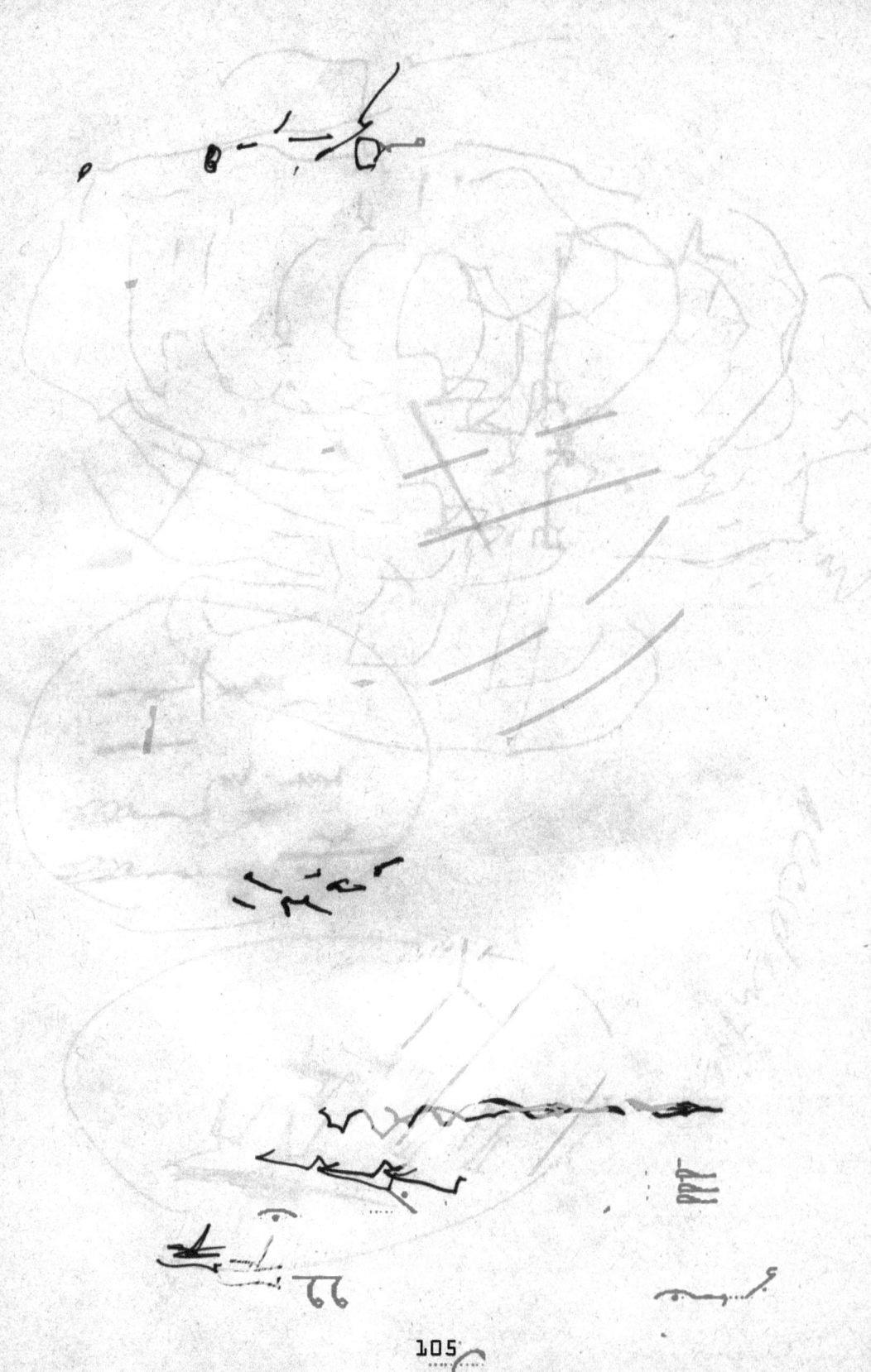

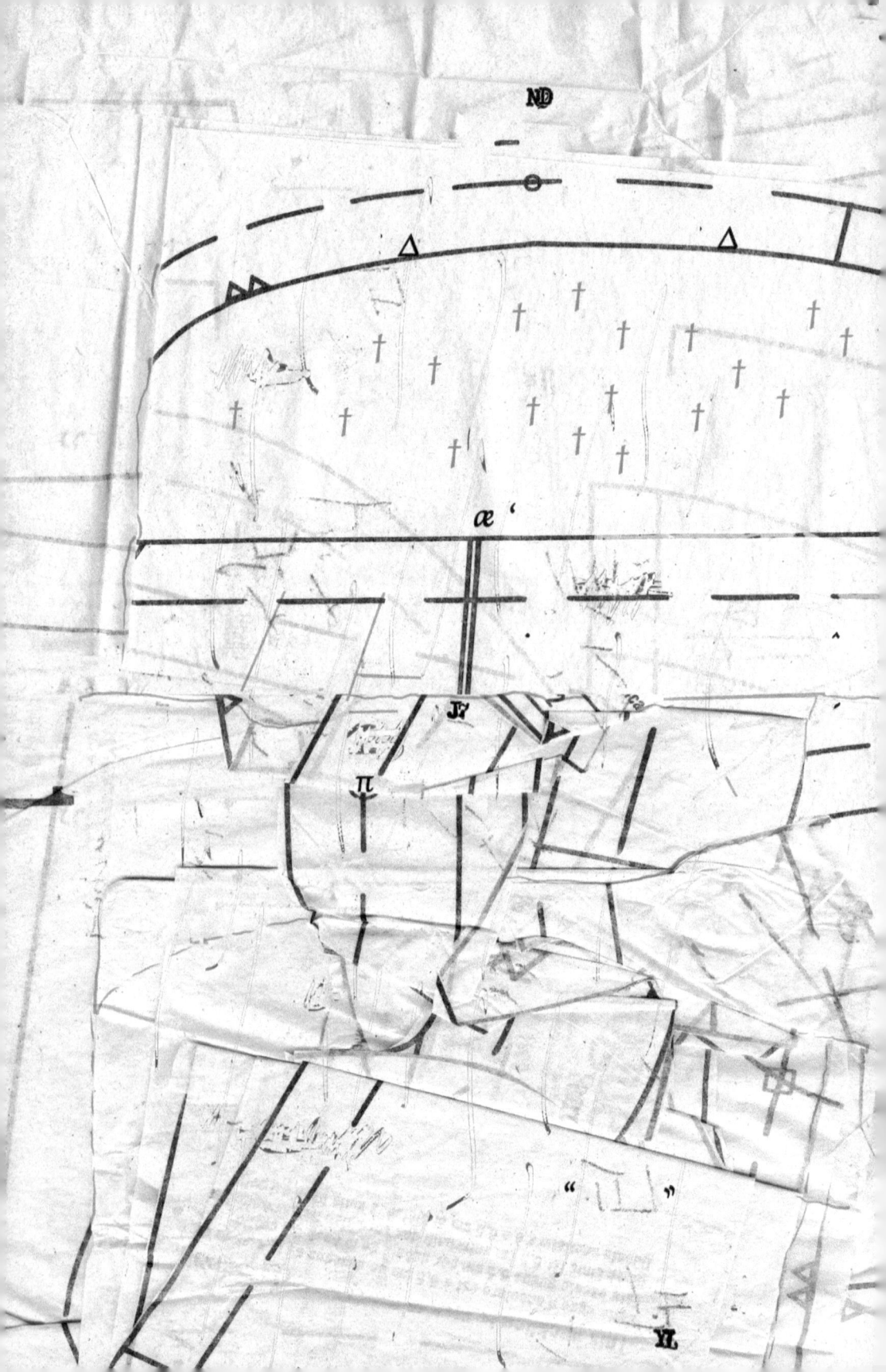

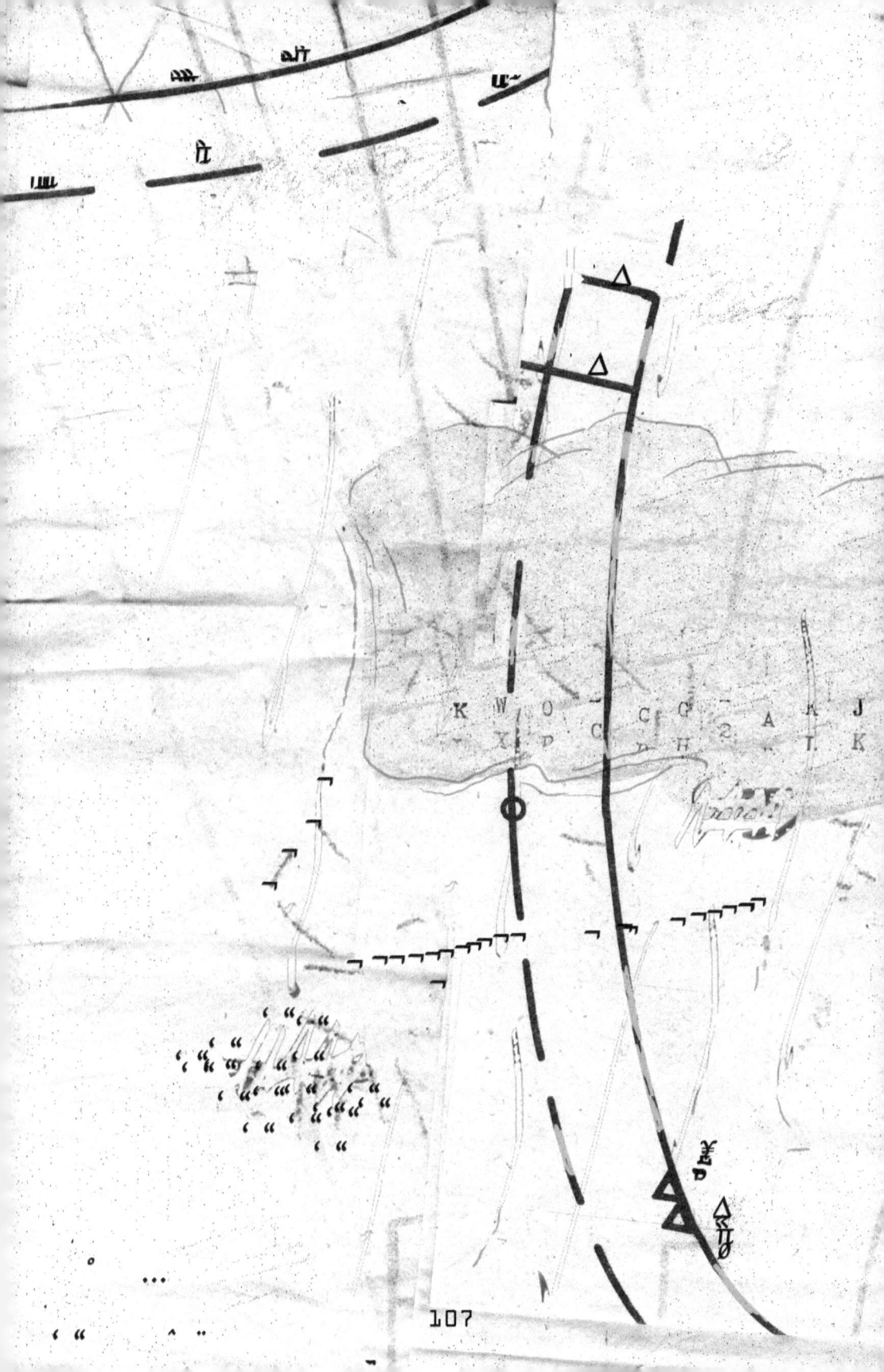

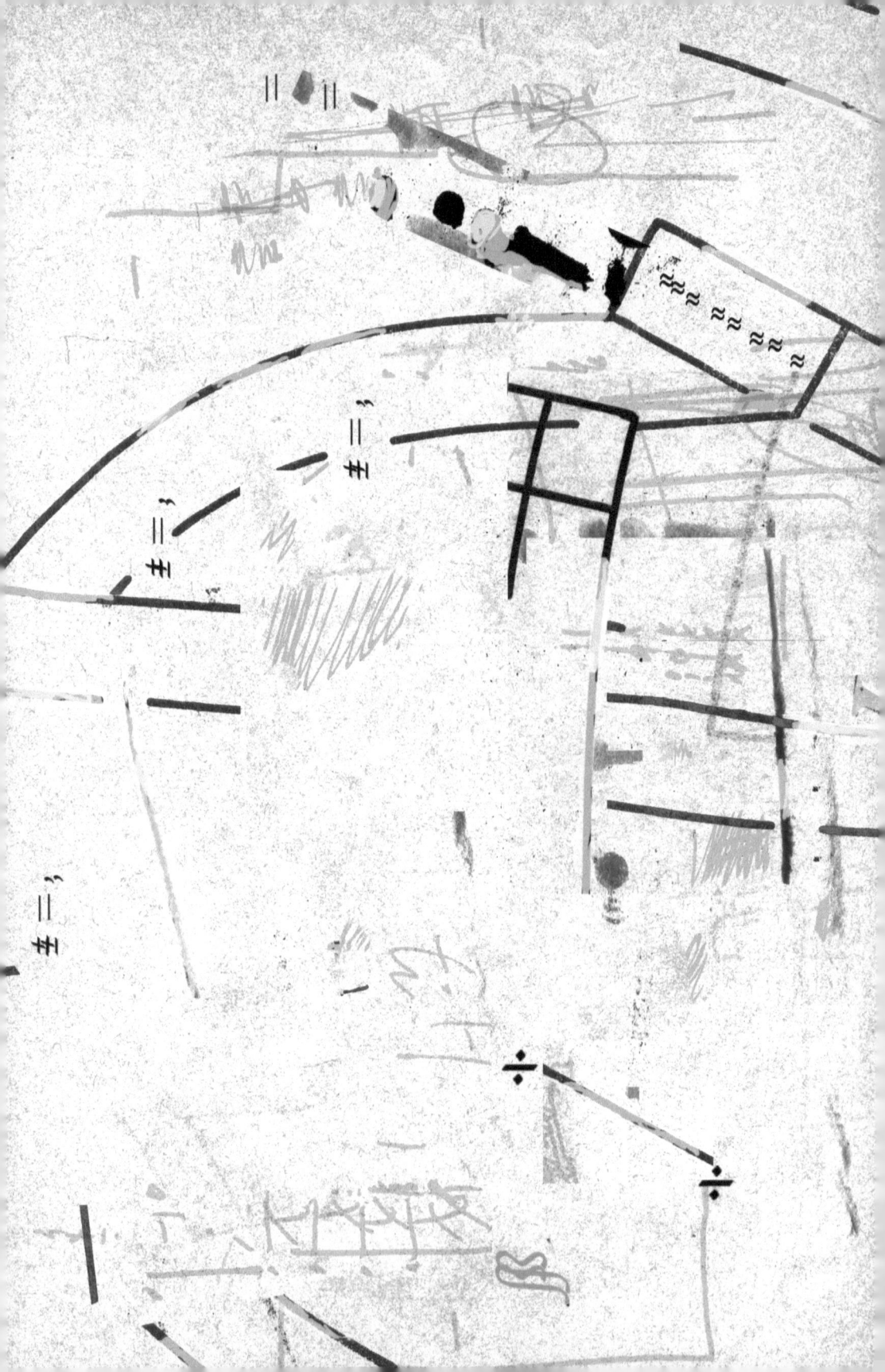

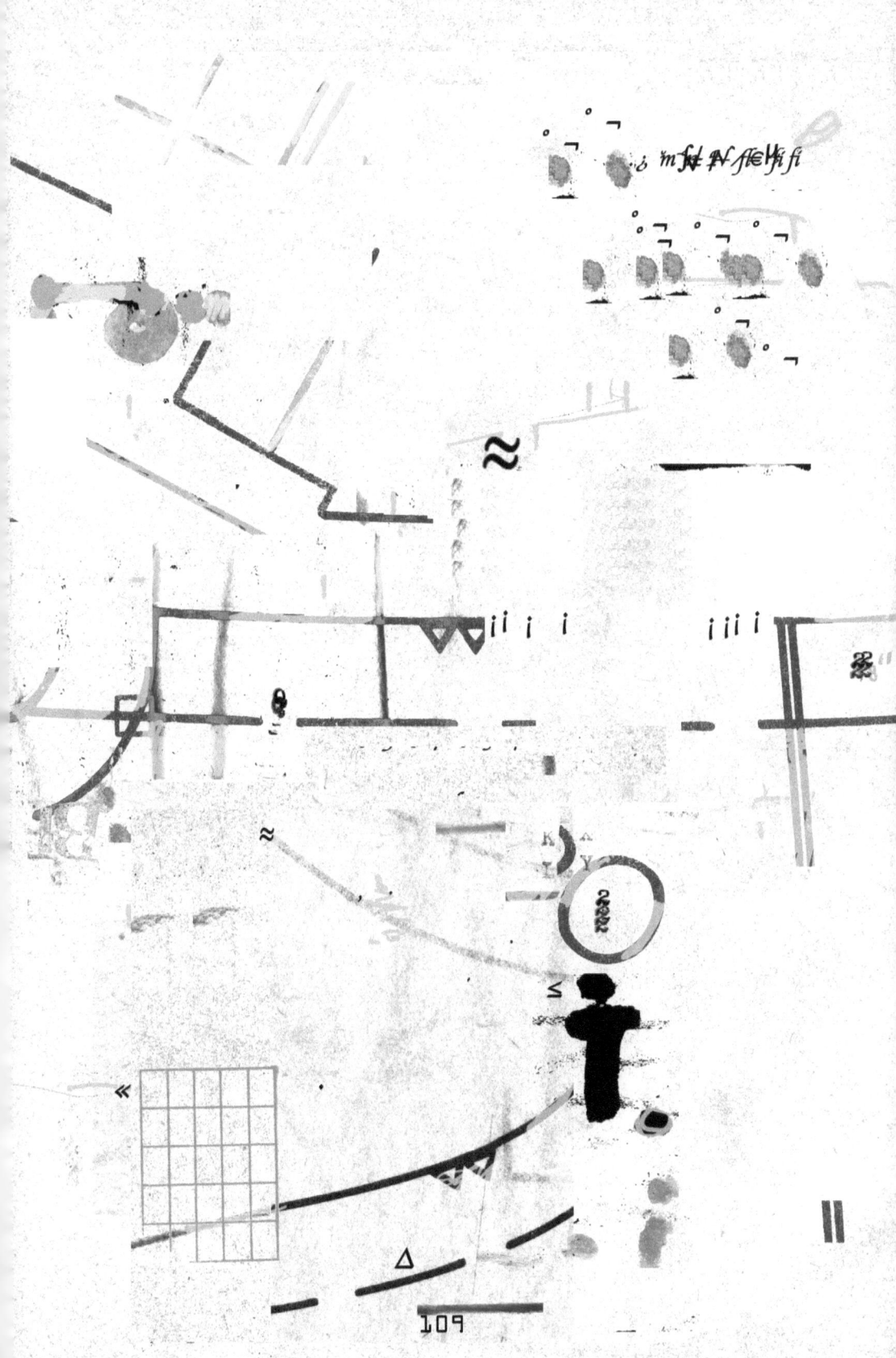

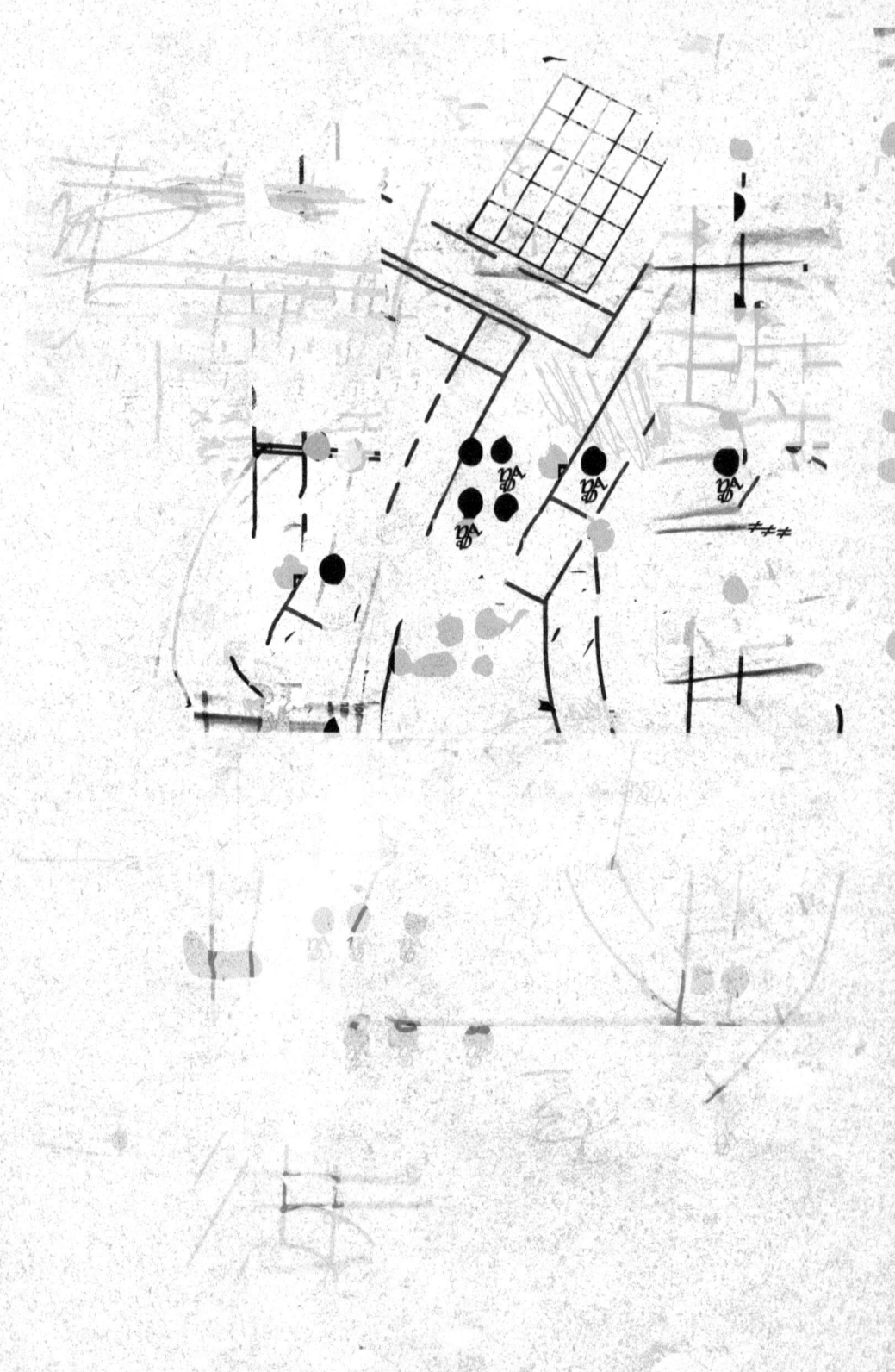

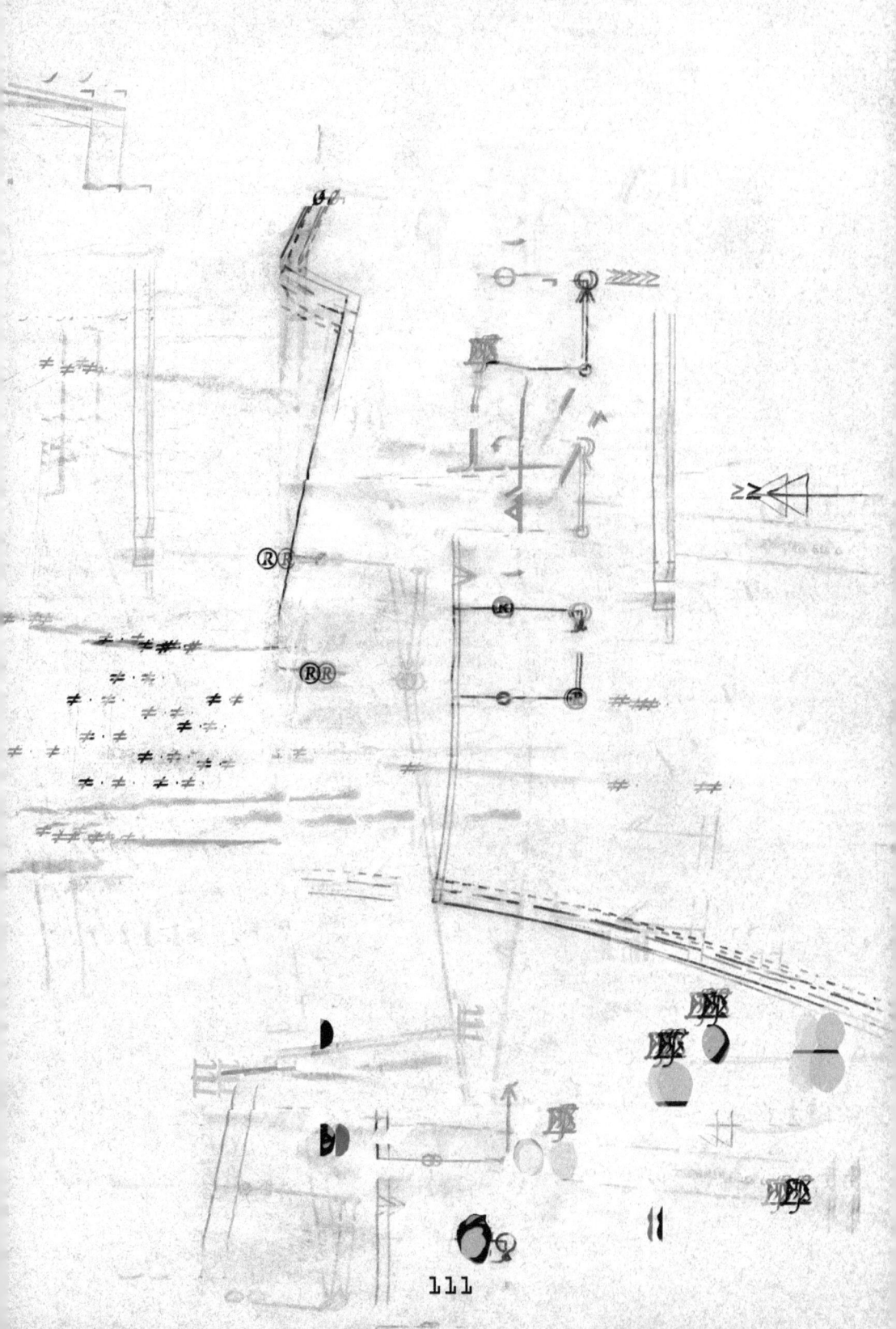

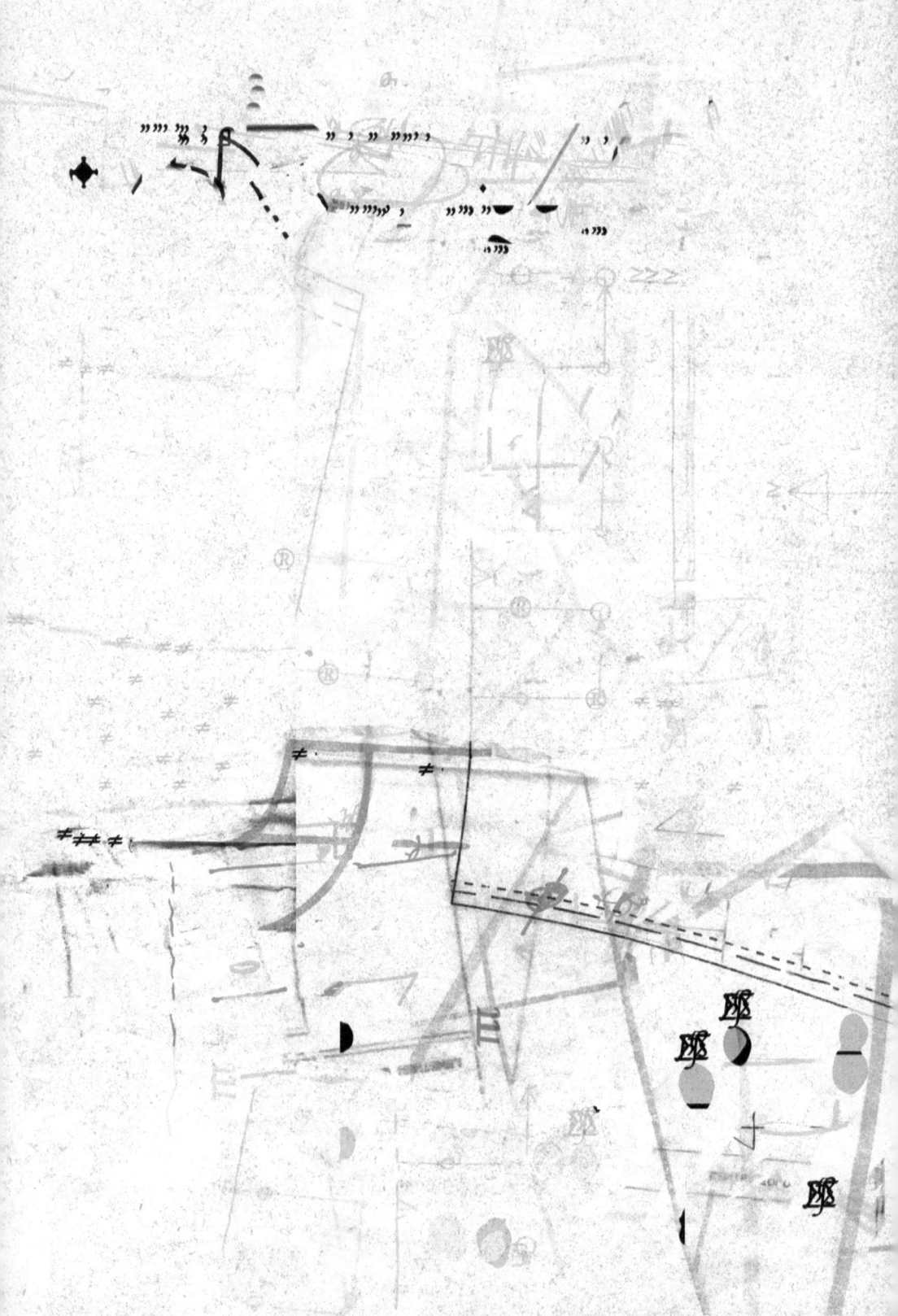

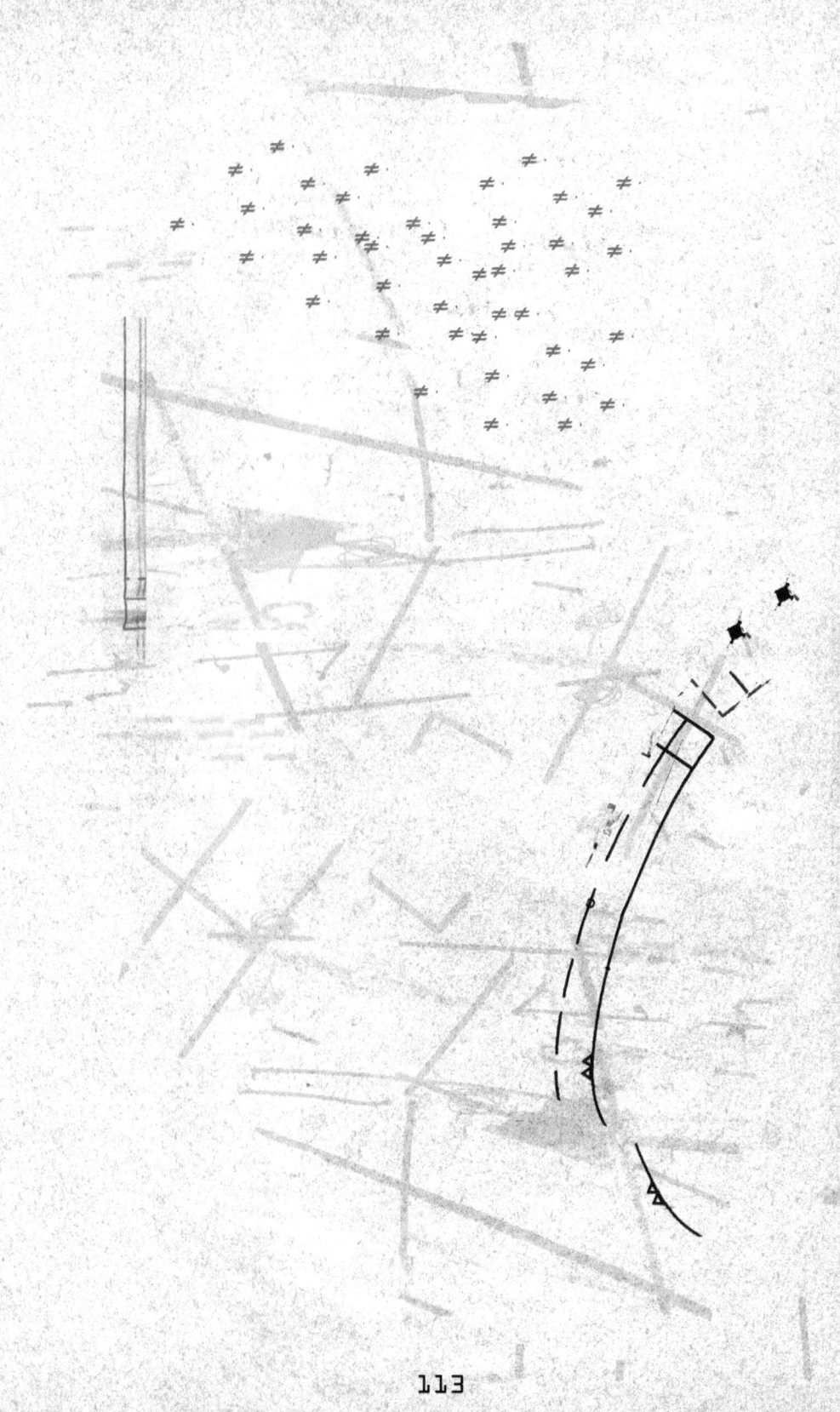

113

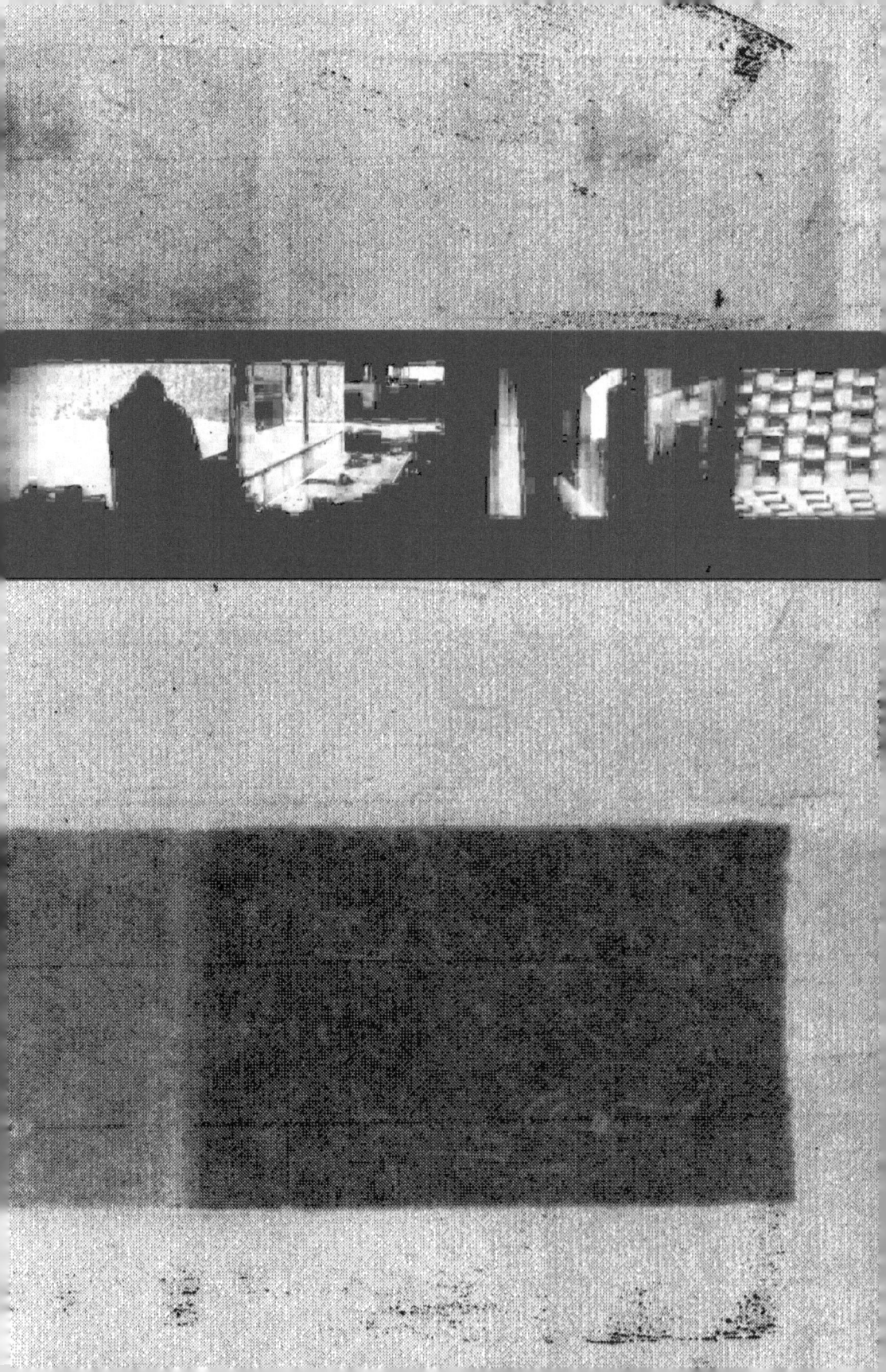

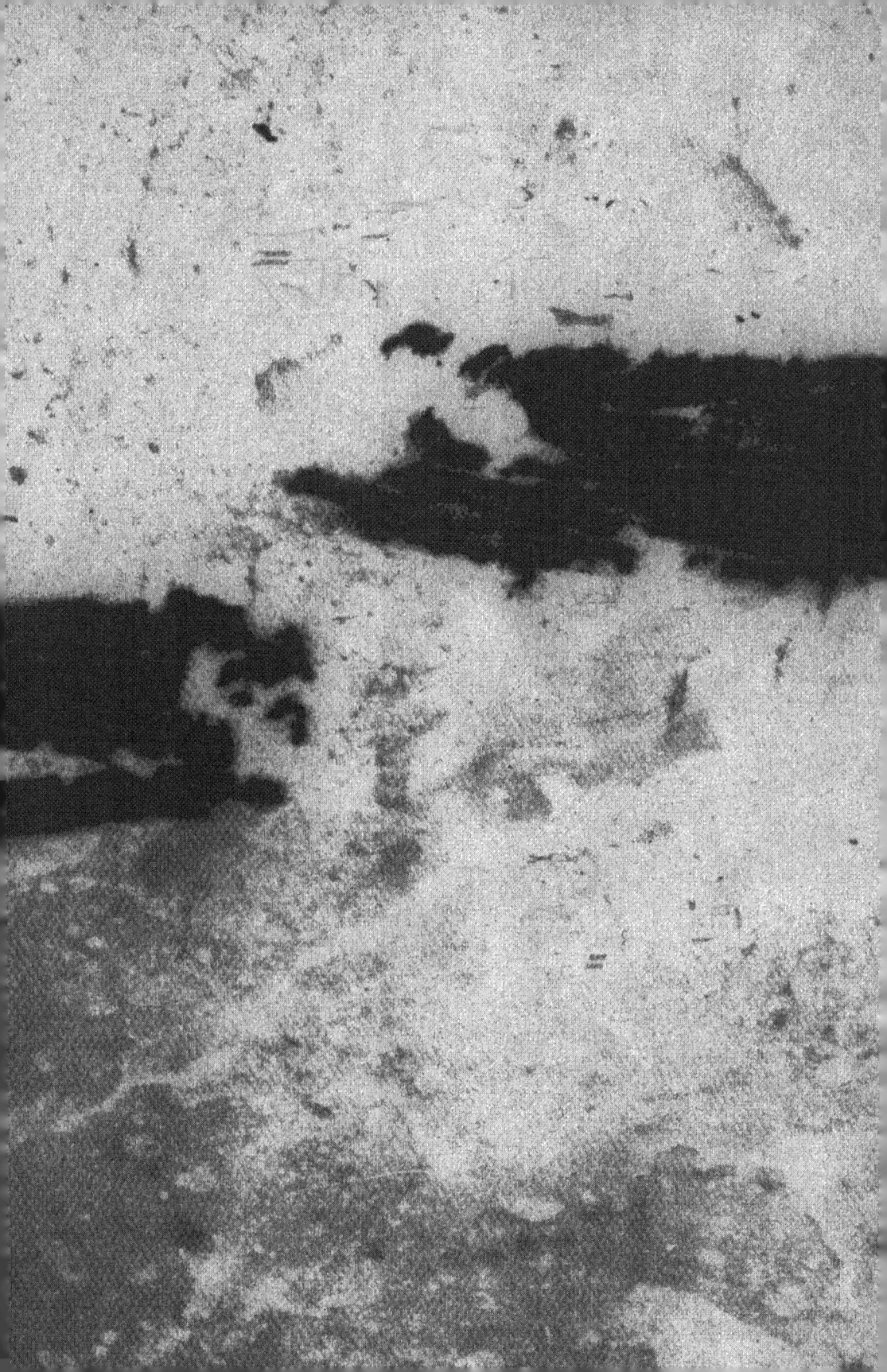

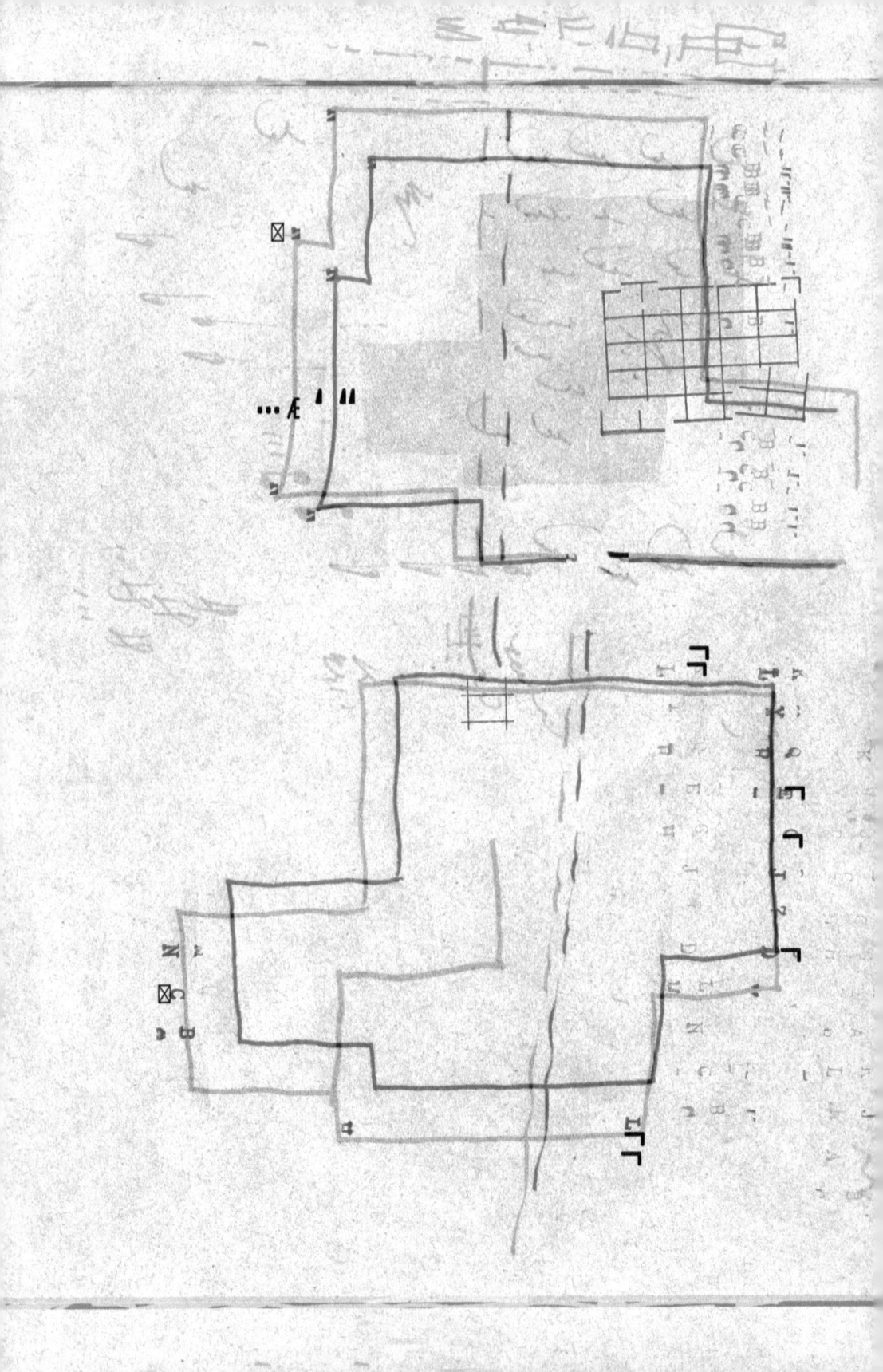

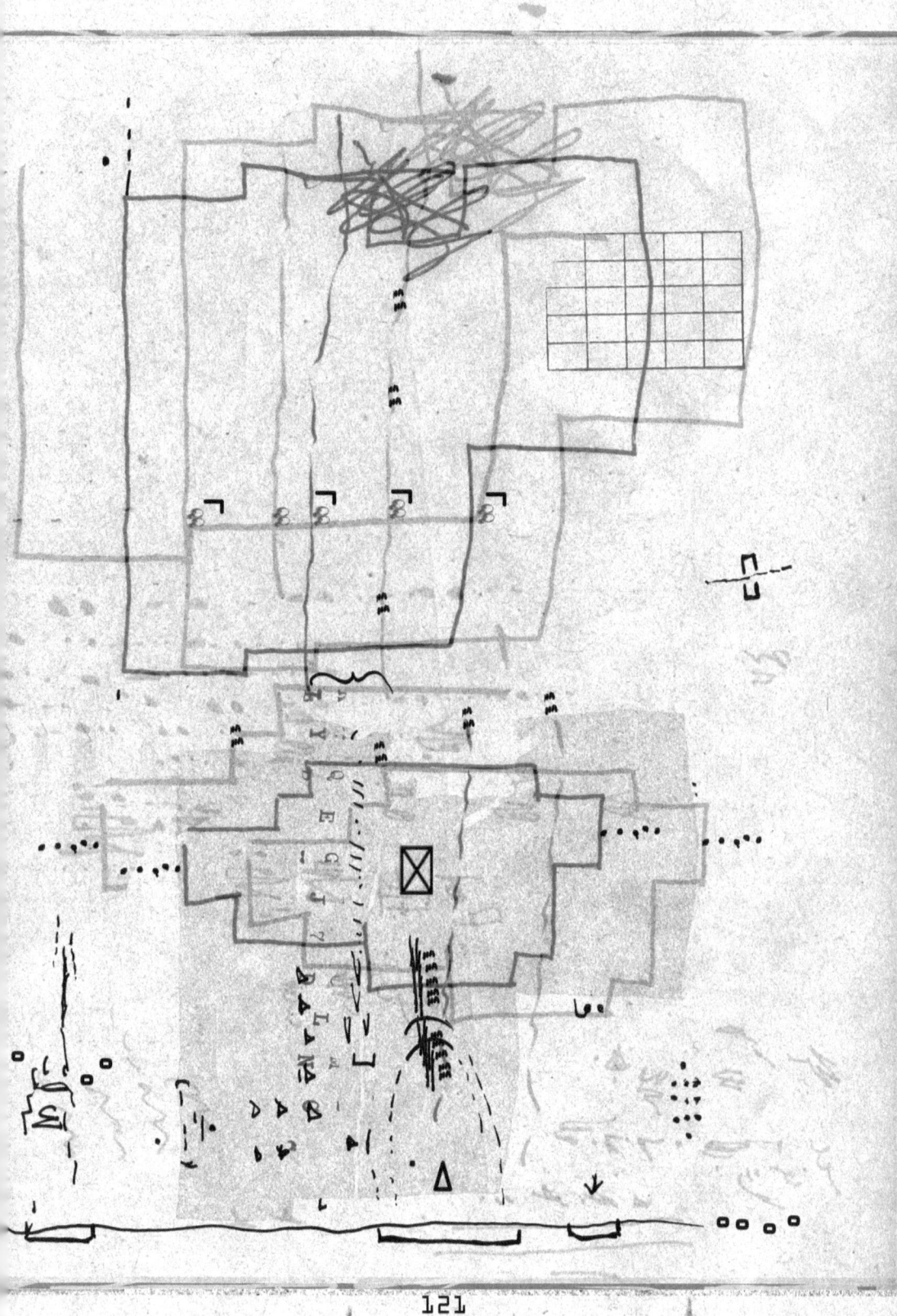

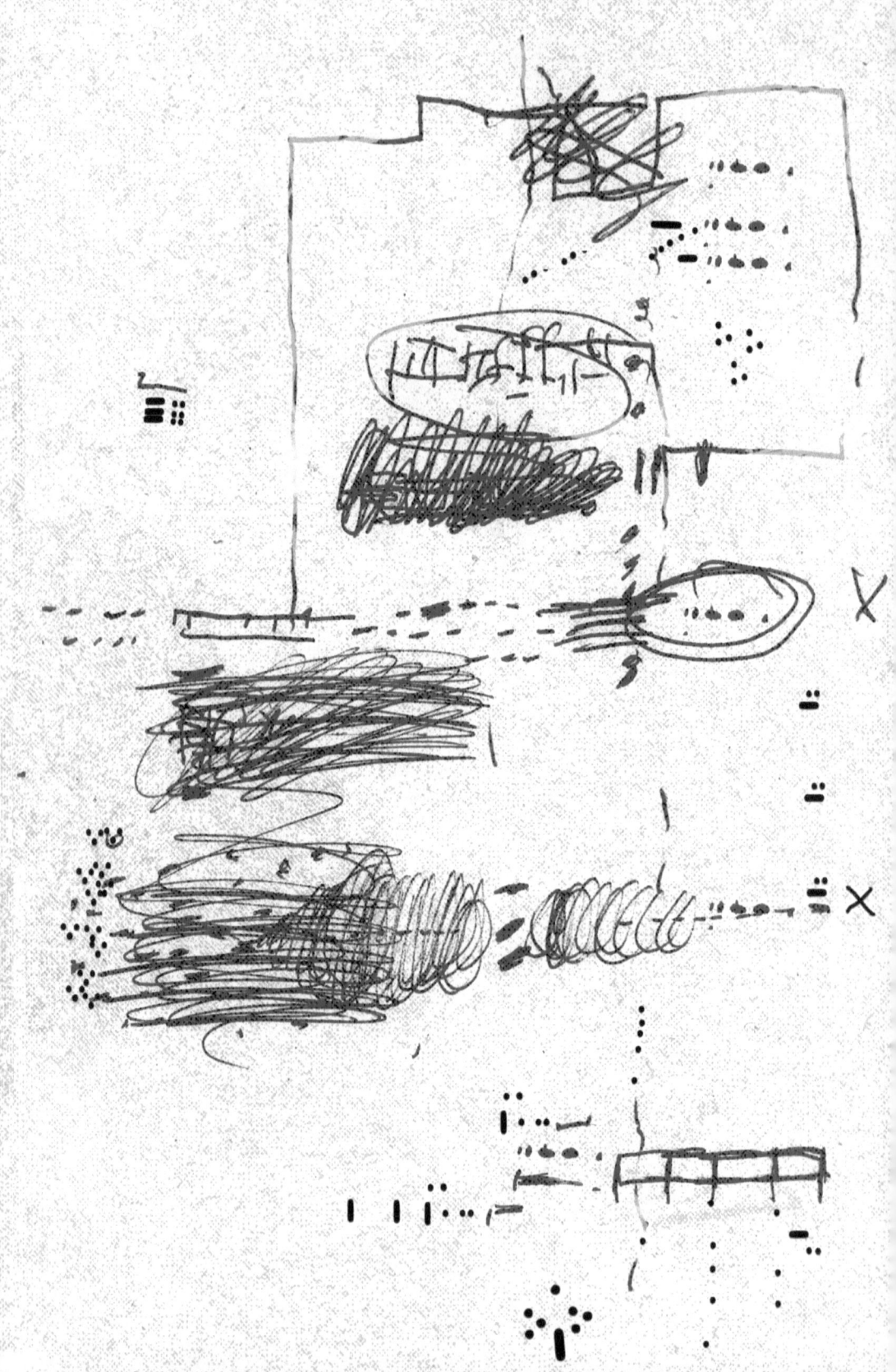

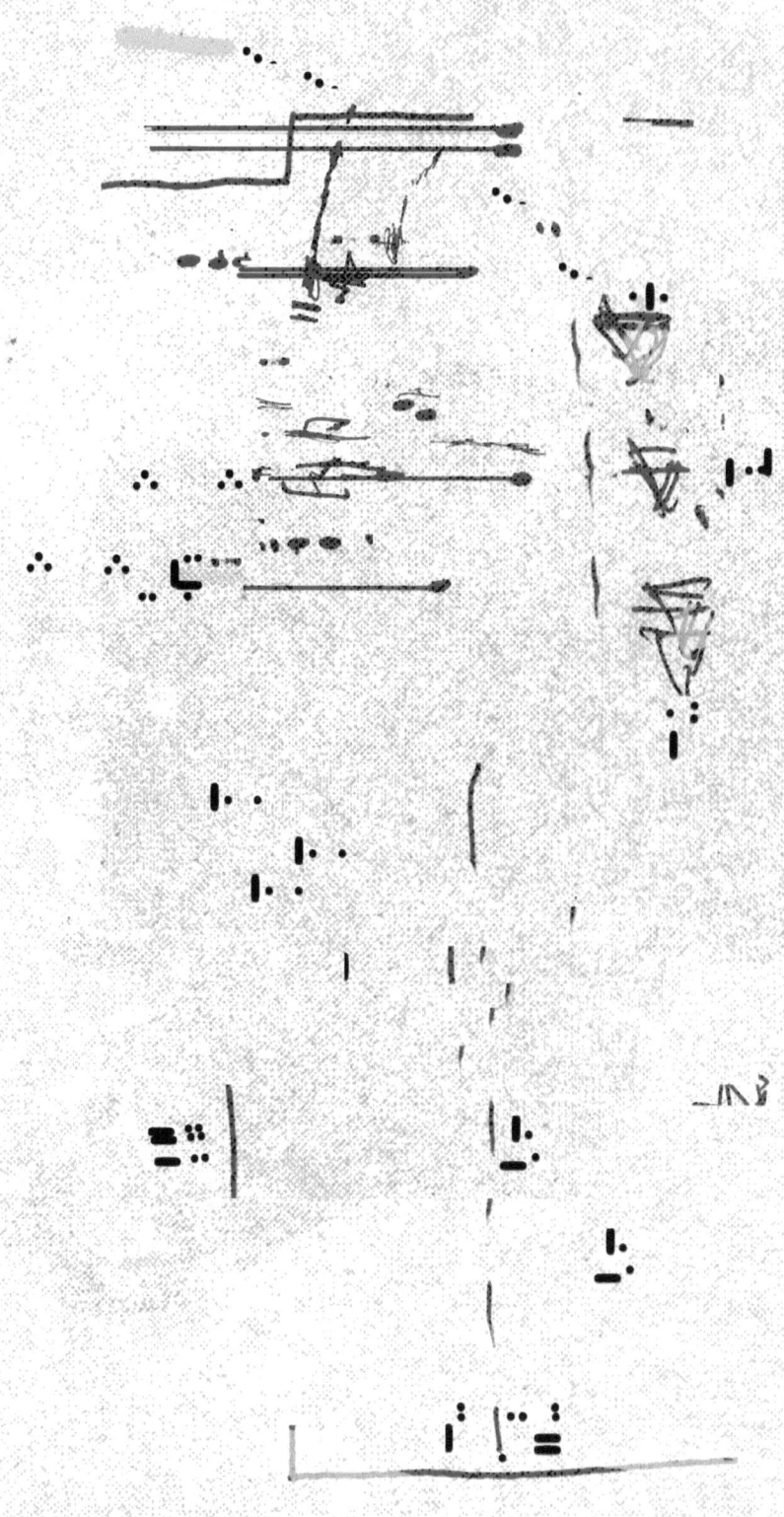

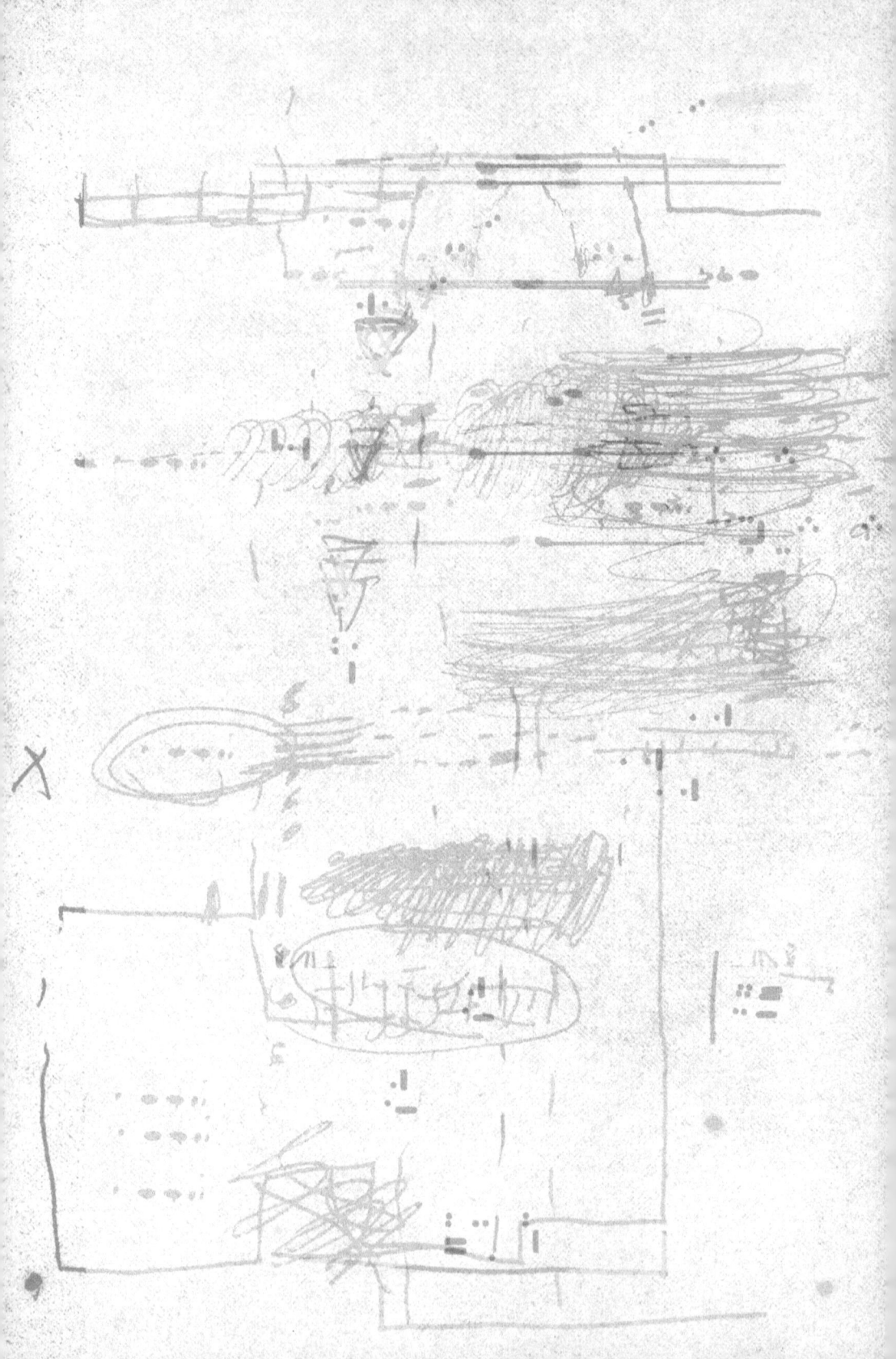

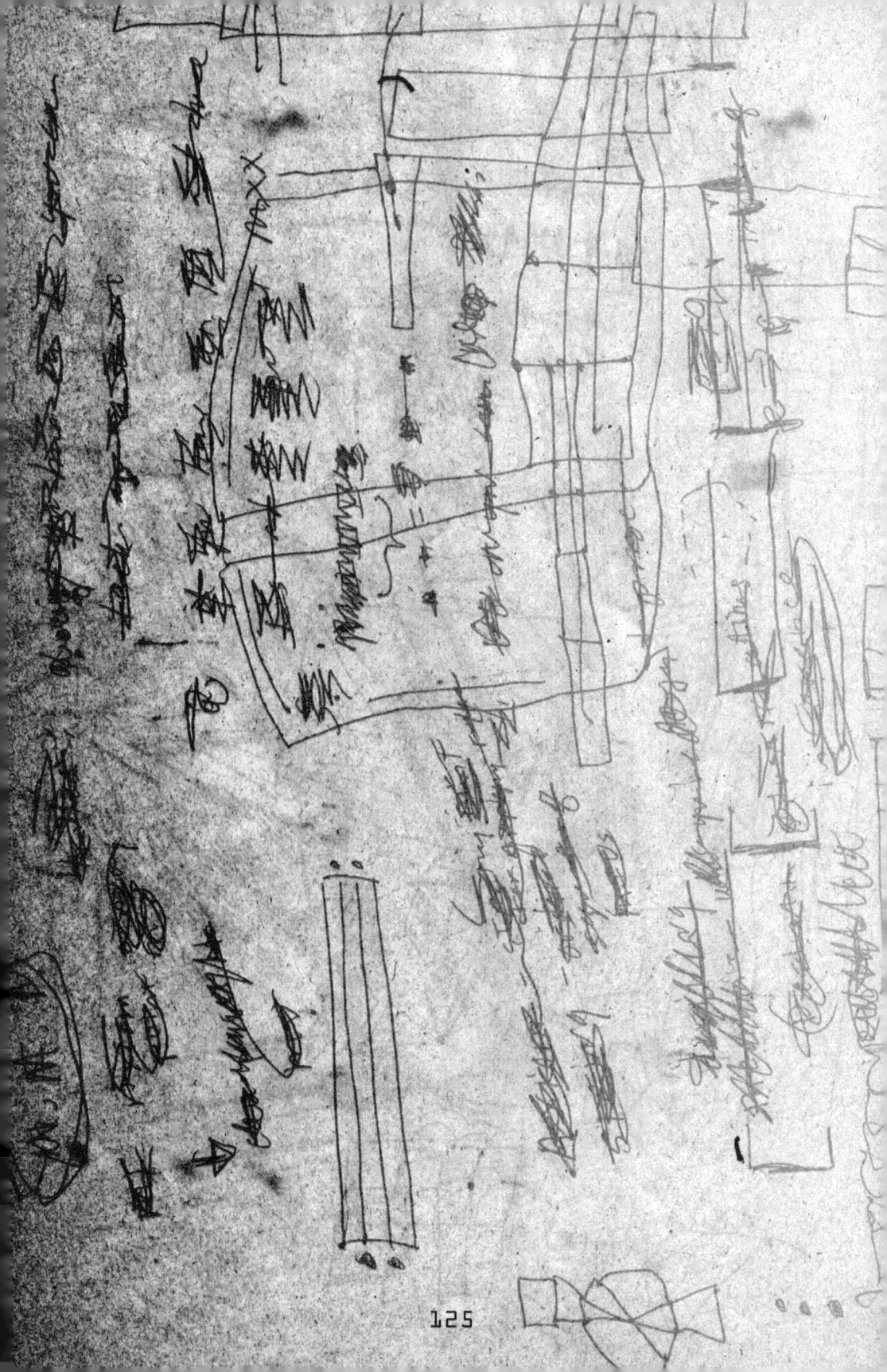

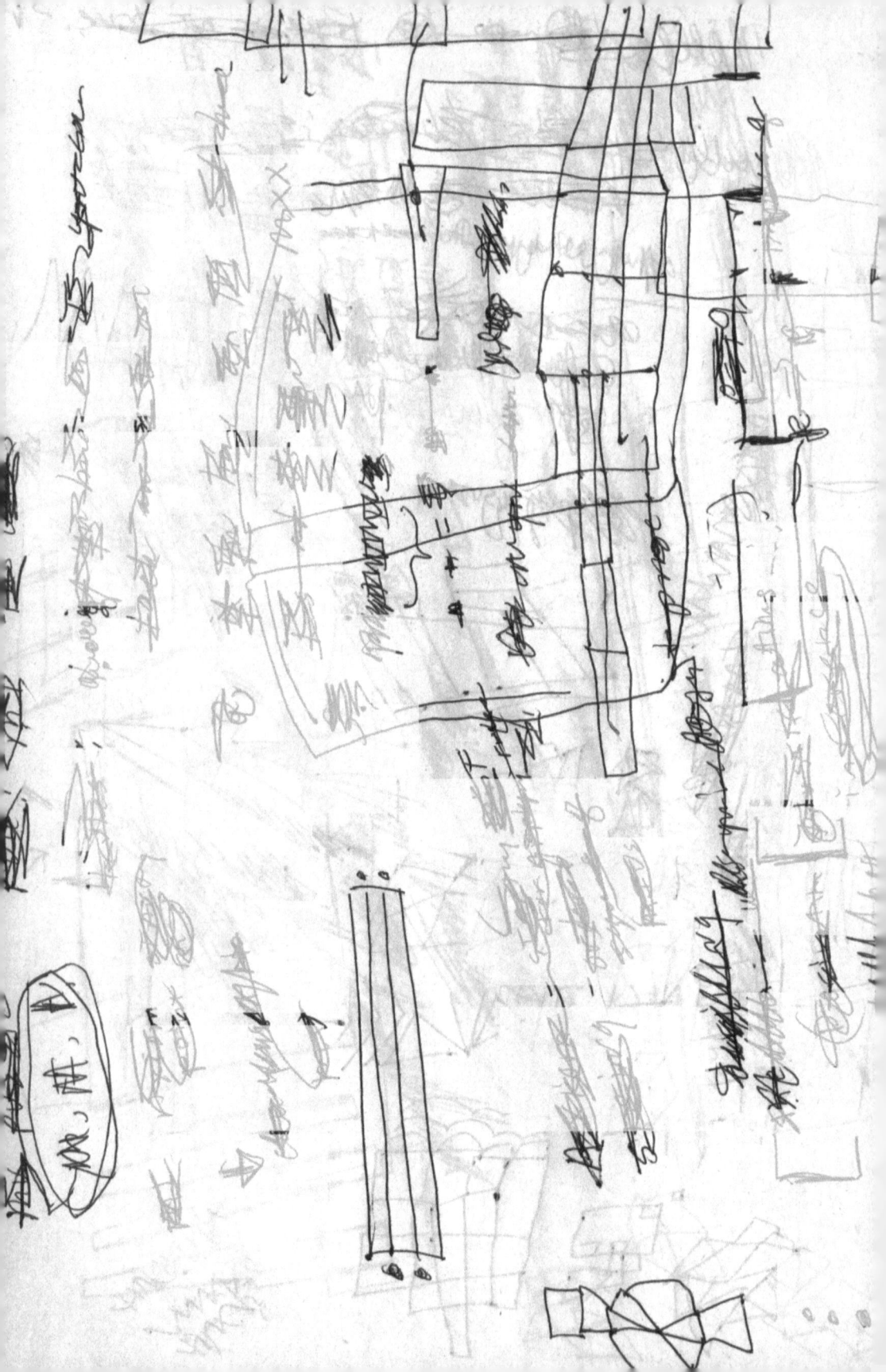

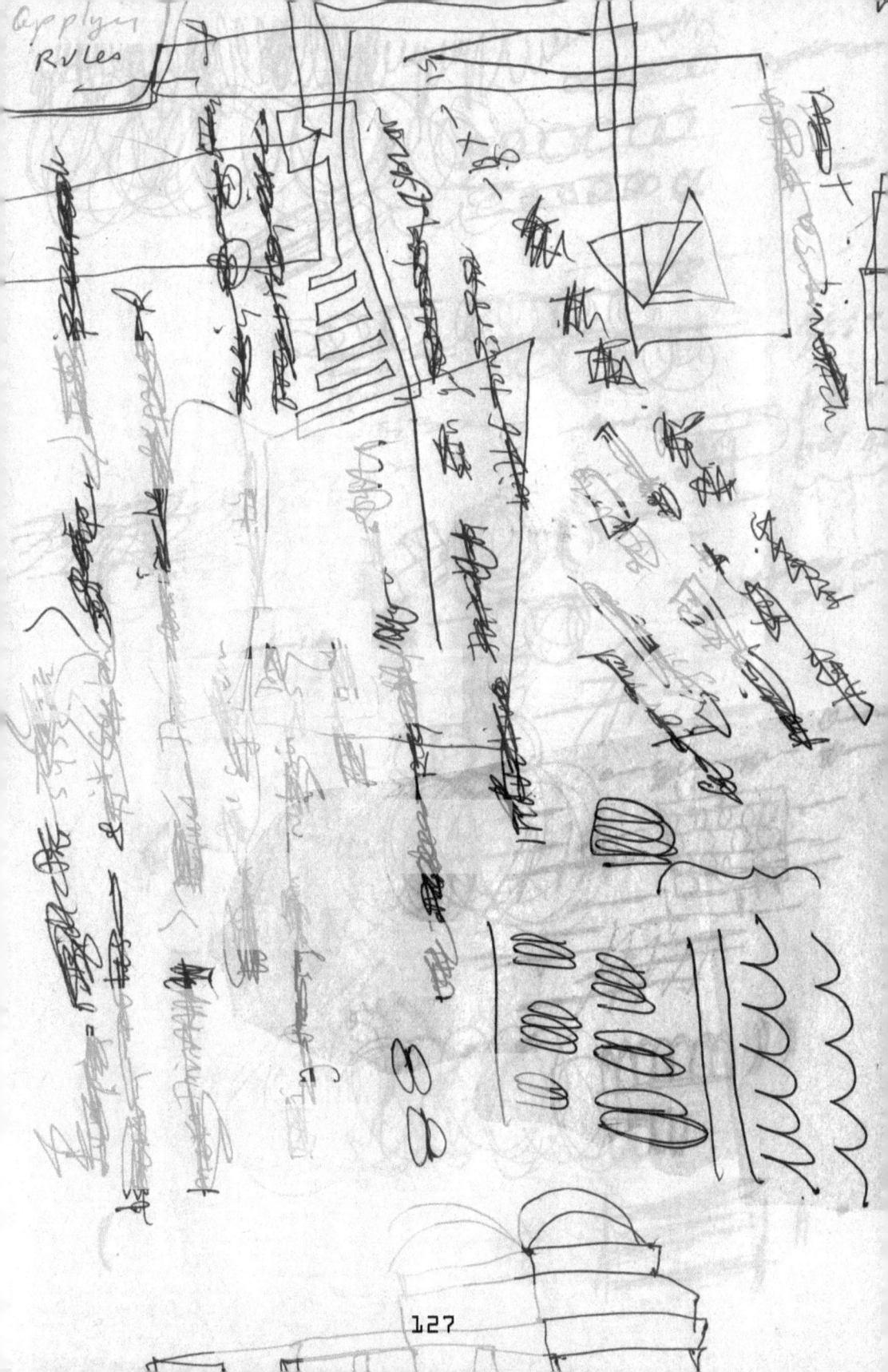

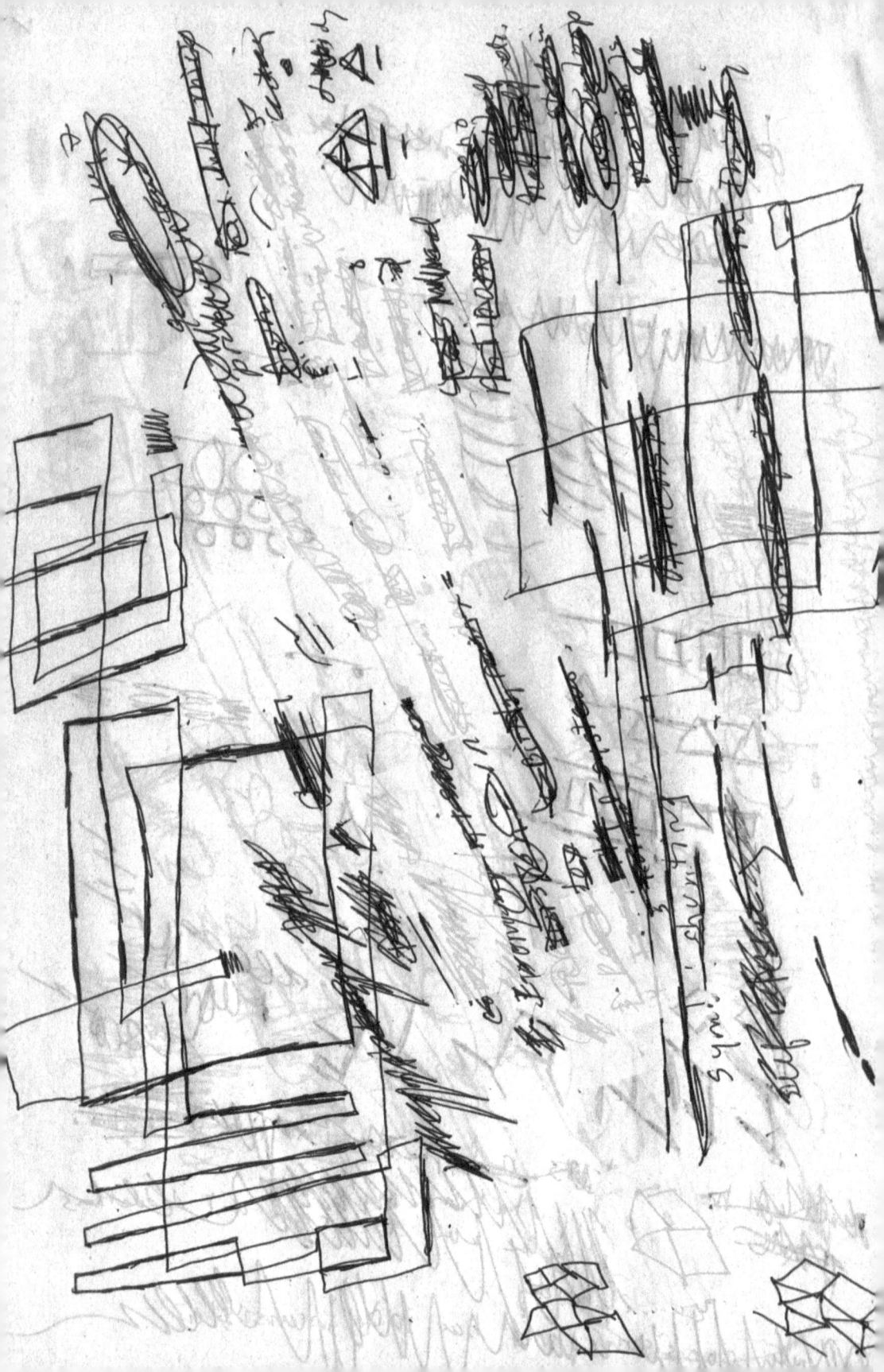

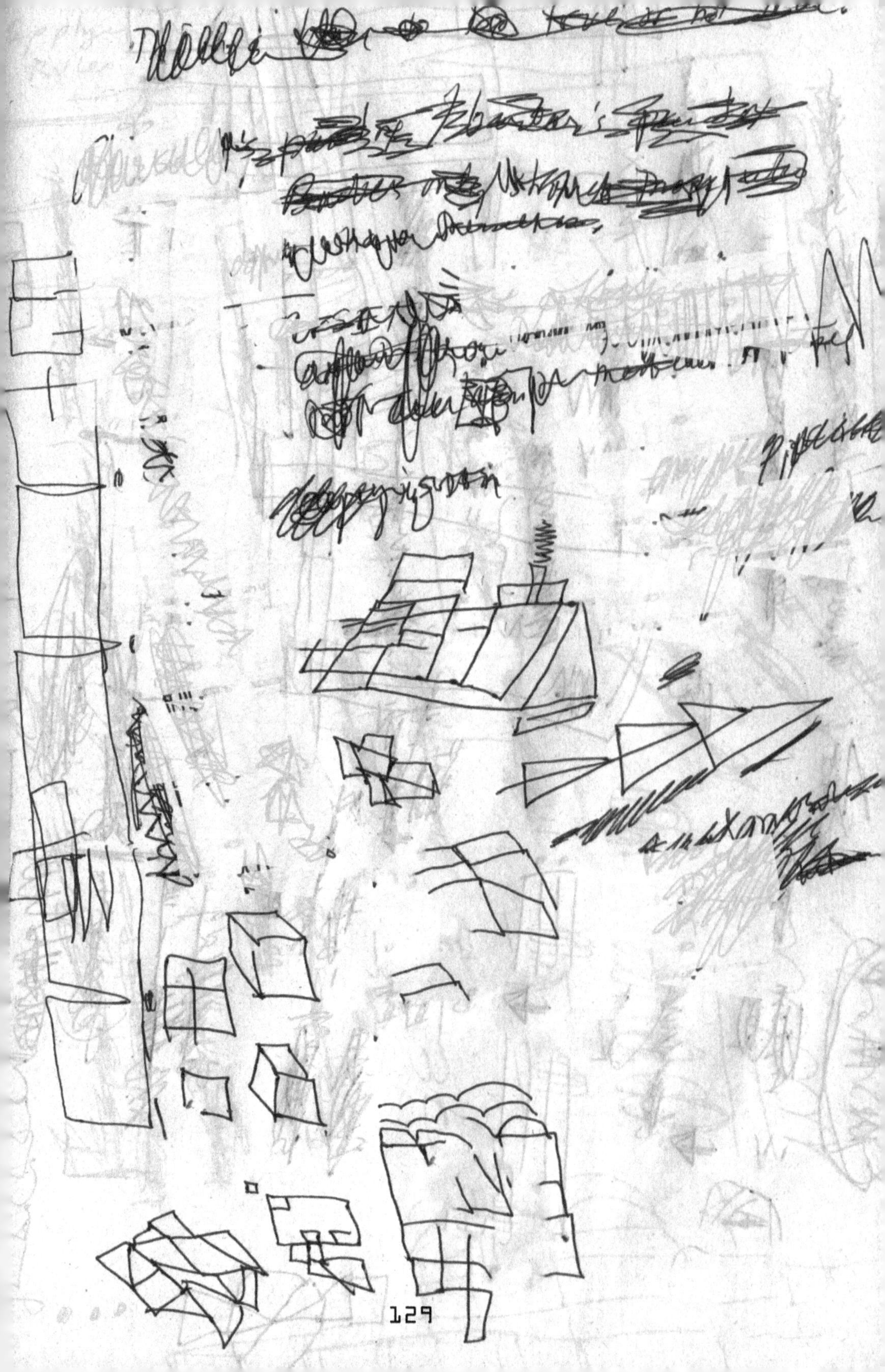

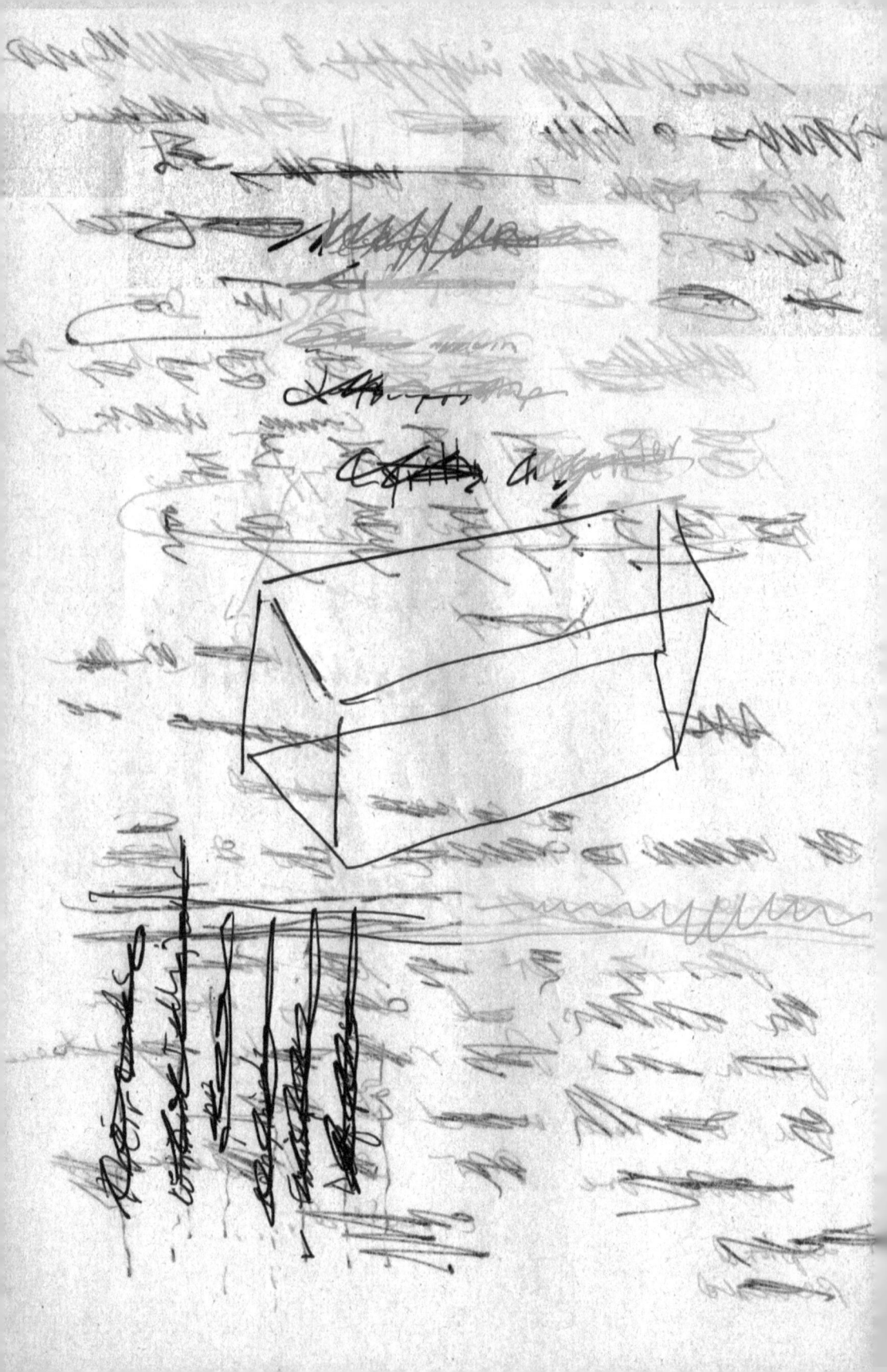

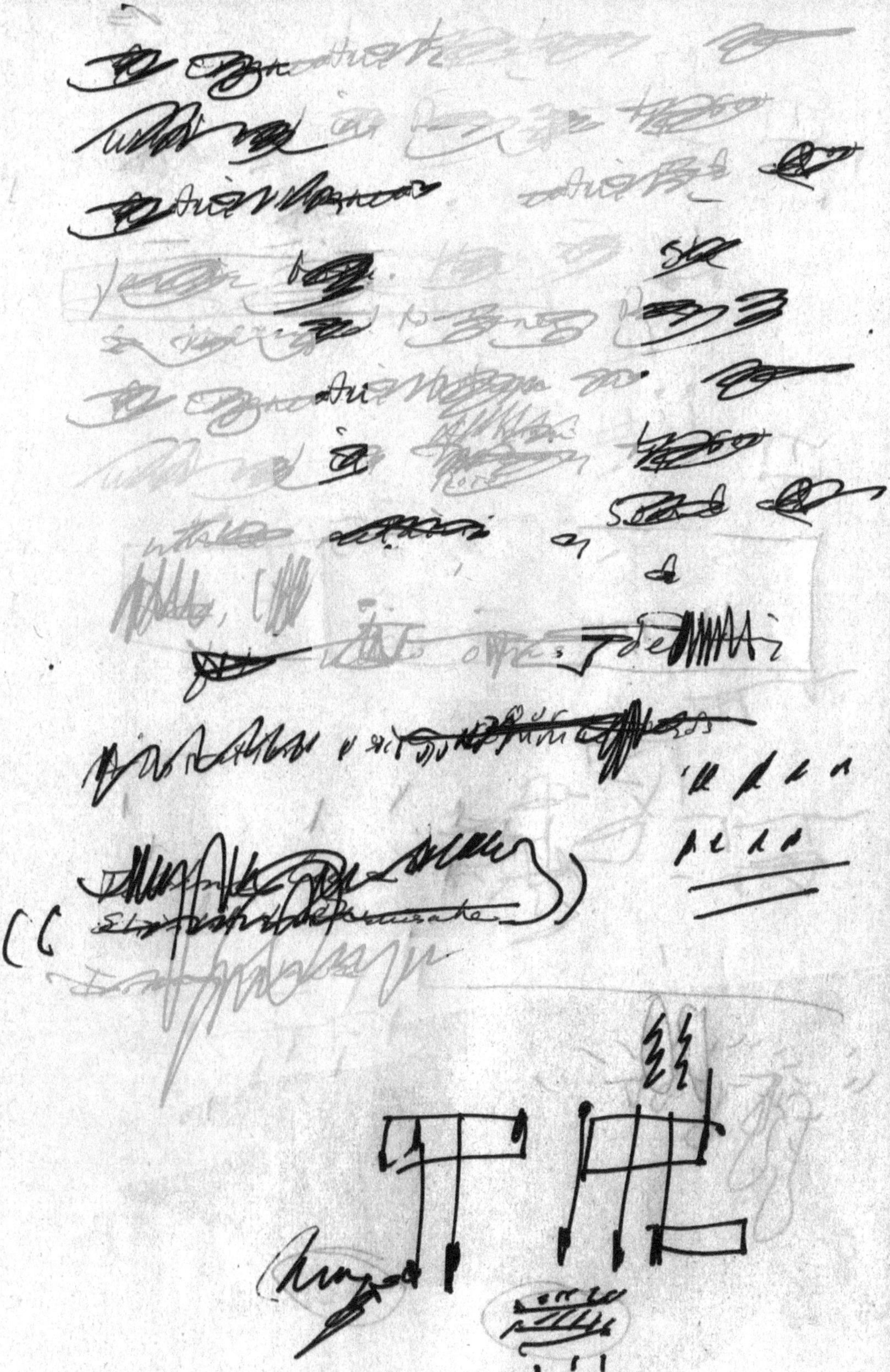

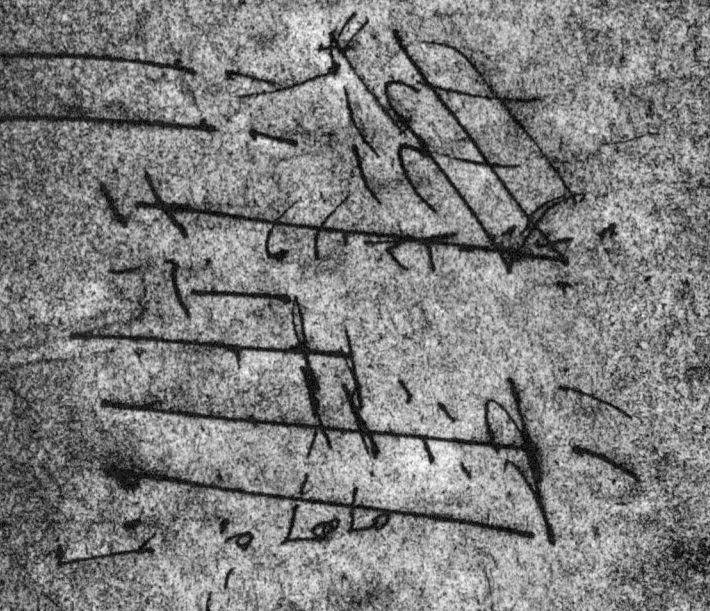
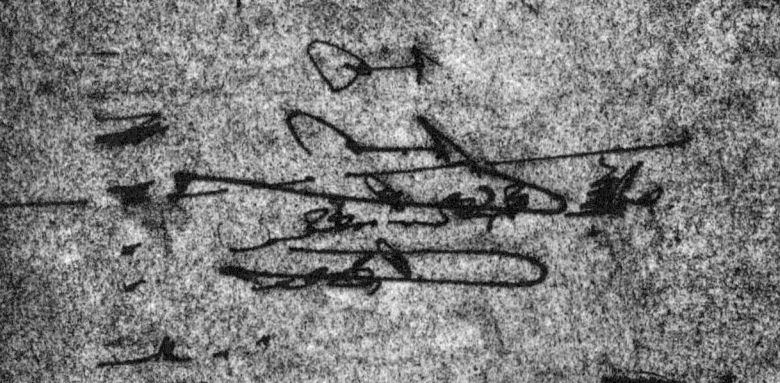
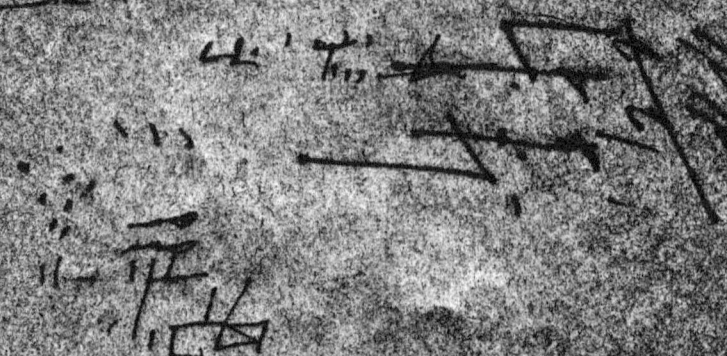

www.ingramcontent.com/pod-product-compliance
Lightning Source LLC
Chambersburg PA
CBHW050454290526
45786CB00006B/2286